TEENAGE WITCH'S BOOK OF SHADOWS

The Teenage Witch's Book of Shadows

By

Anna de Benzelle and Mary Neasham

GREEN
MAGIC

This first edition published in 2001 by
Green Magic
BCM Inspire
London WC1N 3XX

Typeset by Academic and Technical, Bristol
Printed by PMC Printers, London

Cover Design by Chris Render
Cover Artwork © Trystan Mitchell 2001
Technical Assistance R. Gotto and Wes Freeman

ISBN 0 9536631 5 9

GREEN MAGIC

Contents

1

Introduction

What is witchcraft? Is it flying on broomsticks, casting spells, devil worship, or sacrificing the odd virgin at midnight? No sorry, that's not it and if you thought it was then perhaps this book is not for you after all!

Witchcraft today is more about self-empowerment through connections of divine energy using the old pagan traditions. Witches acknowledge, understand and worship the Goddess/ God in everything. We see this as representing the female/male force in life and that it should be equally revered.

Witches also revere nature and our mother Earth, so respect for the environment comes pretty high up on our list of priorities. These days of course it is becoming increasingly difficult to find any truly natural areas. Mankind's ridiculous need to redesign an otherwise perfect planet into some kind of overheated concrete jungle is very worrying indeed to modern witches.

Witches basically work with energy drawn from the spirit world otherwise known as ethereal energy. It is the energy that everything in the physical universe contains too. So you can say that we are energetic beings also. This energy is used for a number of reasons. It can be used for: self-discovery or improve-ment, healing, guidance, divination the list goes on.

Magic, used correctly, is about learning how things really work and how you can use this knowledge and power to influence your chosen path and change your life forever!

There is no black magic as such. The magic is only ever as good or bad as the intention behind it. Whatever you do of course *will* come back on you. Worth remembering I think. Magical work should always be undertaken with a great deal of responsibility but that doesn't mean to say you can't have a laugh of course!

Learning the 'craft' takes time and patience. To make it a little easier we've set out a thirteen step guide on page 3. As you get more involved you will begin to notice a change within yourself. You will never perceive the world in quite the same way ever again. Some witches experience teething problems and crisis of faith from time to time but usually it is just an indication for you to slow down and take stock of your chosen path. There are no shortcuts. You need to grasp the basics first and be patient, it will pay off. You will soon notice yourself integrating your 'craft' into your everyday life fairly easily.

We hope you like our little book and have fun using it.

Be respectful,
Respect all,
Be respected.

Blessed Be.

2

13 Steps to Becoming a Witch

1 Self Respect

It is very important to like yourself as a witch. The whole point of being one is about self-empowerment. If you have a very negative attitude towards yourself you will find it a tough path to go down. Start off by looking at yourself in a mirror, not too closely, you don't want a pore by pore analysis. Smile at your reflection. Tell yourself everyday what a great person you really are. Say to yourself, "I deserve to be happy," "I will be happy," and "I'm happy being me".

2 Revere Nature

Make time to get out into nature. Visit areas of beauty. Look closely at what you see. Really take in all that you see, hear, feel, smell and, if it is safe to do so, then taste. Tasting nature can be dangerous so if in doubt leave it out, or take something nice to eat or drink with you.

3 Intuition

Start to trust your intuition. This is your sixth sense. If for example you have a gut feeling about something, then trust it. Once you start to hand over some control of your life to your higher self everything should start to fall into place as if by magic.

4 Dream Diary

Start to keep a record of your dreams. If there are any recurring dreams there are usually good reasons for them. Depending on the circumstances they can be events you are re-living, a premonition, something you need to deal with or too much food just before bed! Facing your monsters in dream time is a good way of clearing any psychological blockages.

5 The Elements

Become more aware of the elements, *Earth, Air, Fire, Water and Spirit.* Try to keep a balance of them each day.

Earth: gardening, painting, pottery, cleaning, earning money, or anything really that you consider a "down to earth" activity.

Air: Feed your mind, reading, talking, or any medium that allows you to either absorb knowledge or communicate.

Fire: Use up some energy, sport, walking, cycling or even a good rave!

Water: Try to concentrate on only feeling good emotions but don't bottle any of them up. Let them flow. Or you can just indulge in a bath or shower, bath the dog, clean the car, visit a river or the sea.

Spirit: If possible try and set aside a few minutes each day to quietly contemplate or meditate, preferably outside but this is not essential.

6 Seasons

Start to observe the seasons and sabbats. Actually plan to do things to celebrate each one appropriately. Become more aware of how they affect us, and how we respond to them.

7 Moon cycles

Get into a rhythm with the moon's cycles. Ensure that you are doing the right magic for the phase of the moon. When you can see her take a little time appreciating her.

8 Traditions

Explore traditions. Have a good hard look at all the many pagan paths that are open to you. See if any, or maybe one, appeals to you. This is something you may already be feeling drawn to by now. You may not wish to follow any particular tradition and prefer to create your own, that's fine. Each of us is original after all.

9 Group or Solitary

Some witches prefer to keep solitary counsel others like the idea of group work, some combine both.

A warning on covens. It is unlikely that any well-established coven will take you under the age of eighteen. Then there is always the problem of telling the good from the bad. Generally, if a coven seems anxious to take you on and are preoccupied with sex or being naked or seem basically weird, then run, and don't look back! There are dodgy types in all religions and unfortunately paganism is no exception.

Some covens do work naked or "sky clad" but this is a relatively new thing and not to be entered into lightly.

If you really do want to work with others then it is best to join up with a few pagan mates that you already know and trust.

10 Essentials (Kit)

Listen very carefully: **you need nothing.** Now read that again.

You might however like the idea of acquiring some tools. An altar is nice to have as a focal point to work with. What you put on your altar is up to you. As a guide try to represent each of the four elements. It is also a good idea to put a seasonally suitable offering, e.g. Imbolc – daffodils. You may feel the need for a wand, in which case it is best to check out the section on trees in this book before you start. You could prefer an Athame (ritual knife). Remember knives are seen as offensive weapons in the eyes of the law so leave it out of harms way at home and whatever you do never draw blood with it. This will render it useless as a magical tool. Some people like the idea of a ceremonial robe, some don't Again, it's up to you. A chalice is definitely worth having if for no other reason than having something to contain the water. Crystals or stones are great to have on an altar and have endless permutations.

As a rule, remember KISS. Keep it simple, stupid. No offence. Most witches practise at least one form of divination whether it's as simple as scrying into a teacup or as complicated as Tarot. Now is the time to explore that avenue. There are plenty to choose from so you are bound to find something you like.

Once you are fairly accomplished you will soon find your mates all wanting you to read for them.

12 Book of Shadows

Start to keep a book of shadows. This is a secret spiritual diary reserved for you to keep a record of your spiritual journey.

Bit like this one really.

13 Have fun

Do what you will, harm none.

3

Sabbats

As in all belief systems witchcraft has its special days. The Witches' Year is different to the year, as you probably know it.

It is better to think of the year as circular rather than linear.

The pagan **New Year** starts on 1st of November. From here until Yule in December the last of the sap retreats back into mother Earth and hibernation begins. This is the time of the Crone aspect of the Goddess. She allows the death and decay, but also hibernation to take place. The easiest way to think of it is like the energy of all living things being pulled back down into the ground where the cold and frosts of winter cannot hurt it. You may feel the effects of this gradual slowing down as the nights grow shorter yourself. It is a good time to take stock of what you have achieved in all areas of your life over the previous year. Although nature appears to die at this time it is like all death simply a step towards new life and future growth.

The next Sabbat is **Yule**, which occurs on the Winter solstice December 21st the shortest day of the year. It is believed that this is the date Christians adopted as the date for Christ's birth, or thereabouts. This is the birthday of The Sun. It marks the return of longer days to come. We celebrate the shortest day with a feast as a special treat to cheer up the long winter months. It is a good time to spend with family and the giving of presents certainly lifts spirits. Pagans traditionally decorated their houses with evergreens, which remind us that no matter how bad winter can get, life survives regardless. This is traditionally a good time to visit your elderly relatives.

The next Sabbat to look forward to is **Imbolc**. This marks the return of the Maiden aspect of the Goddess. She represents potential new growth. The arrival of the snowdrops and early spring lambs gives us hope for the year ahead. Between now and the Vernal Equinox is the water tide and with this comes the need to face one's self and many inner journeys are travelled. It is also a cleansing tide and a good time for healing and clearing out. This is probably the origins of the "New Years resolutions" and spring cleaning. This is often a traumatic time of year, or feels it anyway.

March 21st marks the spring or **Vernal Equinox**. Easter usually falls around this time but actually refers to the Goddess, Oestre. Eggs are ripening ready for the young, or Horned God to fertilise. The days are now of equal length and life can feel a little tense. Energy levels should start to pick up after this date and many people feel anxious to get new projects started. The *seeds* are sown for the year ahead.

May 1st or traditionally May Day is **Beltane**. The God and Goddess join and their combined energies produce new life. A great time for love spells. This season is strongly associated with fertility and love. A May Queen is selected and paraded through the streets then crowned. Maidens dance around the Maypole winding ribbons as they go. Morris dancers dance for the general fertility of the season. It is a day off work and a day to dance! Alternatively you could just decide to have a Beltane party and enjoy a good old-fashioned flirt!

The next Sabbat is the **Summer Solstice** June 21st & 22nd.

The days are at their longest and it is a Sabbat related to the worship of the Sun or male energy. After this day the Sun begins it's retreat towards shorter days again. These days it receives quite a bit of media attention due to the annual pilgrimage by people all over Britain converging on Stonehenge. Up until last year this was off limits to everyone. However, English Heritage decided to "open the stones" with very few repercussions so hopefully this is a sign of a general softening towards Pagans in this country, and not before time. It is a good Sabbat for healing and improving your luck.

We are now deep into summer and **Lammas** arrives on August 1st. This is the arrival of the Mother aspect of the Goddess. She is now rich with the fruit of the Beltane union. This marks the start of the harvest. This is a time for reaping what you have sown. Exam results come in. The nights begin to shorten it is a good time to get unfinished projects or tasks completed.

After Lammas we have the **Autumnal Equinox** September 21st. The tides get higher and days start to shorten. The harvest is finished and its time for a rest. Tensions can mount however as we run around trying to make the most of the evening light and warm weather before Samhain arrives.

Samhain is 31st October and as a day it doesn't really exist. It is the day of the dead. A day to remember your loved ones who have departed. It is also called All Hallows Eve. All souls day. This is a day for the spirit world. Although ritual work is best avoided on this day divination is fine. It is the last day of the old year and of course another good chance for a party.

When you start out on your magical path it is probably better to avoid working on Sabbats and just stick to the appropriate moon cycle instead. Sabbats can prove a little overpowering at first.

4

Moon Magic

The moon has a great deal of importance in magic and in witchcraft in particular.

In magic, the moon governs the subconscious mind, which is where all magic is brought from the idea (air), the desire to make it happen and the actions needed (fire) to the subconscious, which is where inner forms are built (water) before being brought into the physical world of here and now (earth). It all seems quite easy when you write it down but it does take a bit of practice to make it work.

The best way to approach moon magic is first of all, to become aware of where the moon is in its cycle and what these different cycles mean.

The moon has a 28 day cycle which means that there are 13 full moons per year. You will find that there are a lot of different systems of naming the various moons. Some people go by the Chinese system, some use the Norse system and some people use either a vaguely Celtic system or even North American. As it doesn't make any difference to the moon, it seems to us to be sensible to follow whichever type of magic you are interested in. If you haven't yet quite made up your mind, then a good way might be to classify the moons, if you need to, by the seasons.

So, working from the Vernal (or Spring) Equinox, which is about the 21st of March, to the Summer Solstice, around 21st of June, you are in the Fire tide when everything is growing. There is a lot of fiery energy around and it is a dynamic time when you can start lots of new projects and have the energy to get them off the ground. So your moons will be fiery moons and you can give them appropriate names. The fire tide whilst necessary for getting things moving can be an aggressive time. Watch out for loony arguments.

From the Summer Solstice to the Autumnal Equinox (around 21st September) you will be in the Earth tide which is the tide of fruition, when what you planted, or started in the Fire tide, should produce a result. So as you move towards the end of the Earth tide you should start to gather a harvest from your earlier efforts. The moons will be earth moons, rather slower in tempo than the fire moons and with a heavier, more voluptuous feeling.

The time from the Autumnal Equinox to the Winter Solstice, which is about 21st December, is the Air tide and this is a good time for planning, collecting information and making preparations. The Air tide is very unstable, a time for making magic but hold on to your hat or it may get blown off rather suddenly.

From the Winter Solstice to the Vernal Equinox is the Water tide. This is known as the Cleansing tide. It is the time of the year when nothing is growing above ground but things may well be stirring underneath. It is thought to be the best time for clearing out unwanted or unnecessary baggage. This applies to things as well as to habits, silly ideas and anything else that is collecting in your life and holding you back.

So what do you do with a moon cycle? Each moon phase is divided into New, Waxing, Full, Waning and back to New again.

On the whole the New Moon, which is invisible on the day that it occurs, is not a good time for doing magic. Some intrepid souls may like to try but they either get nowhere or achieve results they don't like. It is best left alone.

As the moon waxes, or grows more visible, the energy is a rising, positive one, which is very useful for achieving improvements, starting things, creating and doing healing work.

As you get up to the Full Moon the emotional level tends to become a bit unstable so if you feel either a bit hyped up or you fly off the handle for no reason, that *is* the reason. It is a time of fruition, when things that were started in a waxing phase, not necessarily the one immediately before the Full moon, will come to a completion. It is best not to start new work at the Full moon as it may well go off in all sorts of directions. Use it for celebrating your achievements, consolidating or moving an already established project into a different direction. The week before a Full Moon is a good time for giving a big boost to situations that are slow moving or stuck.

The Waning moon is often regarded as an unlucky time or a 'bad' time. It is nothing of the sort. It is the time for clearing up, cleaning out, getting rid of things or putting them away. This can be magical work as well as physical. So if you want to get rid of a habit you don't like, work on it in the Waning moon. Healing can also be done in the Waning moon, work on getting rid of the problem. For instance if a friend has an infection you could do a working to make it to dwindle away and then in the next waxing moon do some work to build them up and make them feel better, thus shortening their convalescence.

Bear in mind that healing work for someone else should only be done with their consent. It is interfering of the worst sort to decide that you will heal someone without getting their agreement first. If they find out they may well be very angry with you. It is very important to remember that you don't know why they are ill. It may be that it is to do with their karma and they may have to face and sort out aspects of themselves that they don't like. Possibly their Higher Self has been working away on this for ages, finally gets them to a point where they *have* to look at a particular situation and you come along and ruin it by imposing healing – all with the best of intentions but without knowing the background. So ask first. Usually people will be glad to be offered a helping hand, if they know what is being done.

Then you find yourself back at the next New moon. The really good thing about it from the magical point of view is that you don't have to wait very long if you need a particular moon phase for some work.

When you start to connect with the moon in all its phases you may well find that your menstrual cycle begins to fit in with the moon's cycle too. Sometimes this doesn't happen or something happens in life which knocks everything off course. If you need to get back into a regular cycle try sleeping with the curtains open and the moon shining into your bedroom. It shouldn't take more than three or four months to get things back to normal again. The rhythms of the moon affect us all very deeply, as our bodies are made up of large amounts of water which responds to the moon's magnetic pull even inside us.

Many witches worship the Moon in all its phases as manifestations of the Great Goddess and will have ceremonies at each phase or else at the New and Full moons to celebrate her changing aspects.

There are all sorts of superstitions associated with the New Moon, for instance not looking at the New Moon through glass or in the mirror as they are supposed to bring bad luck. There is also the old country idea that you should go out to greet the New Moon and, bowing to it three times, turn the money over in your pocket. To do this successfully you have to do it on the first night that the New moon is visible, it should be a thin silver sickle in the sky. It is no good if there are clouds and you must make sure that you have some silver coins in your pocket to turn. It is meant to bring you prosperity for that whole moon cycle.

If you want to do a bit of moon worship, you don't really need any equipment, unless it makes it easier for you. All you need is to be able to see the moon at the various phases, so access to a garden, or a window facing the right way are important. Make sure you are on your own at the time. Then all you need to do is to go out, look at the moon and make a connection in your mind. Use whichever image you have of the inner meaning of the Moon Goddess, greet her and talk to her. She is really very friendly.

5

Colours

Witches have always been aware of the magical significance of colours. From the basic observations in nature they have gathered their knowledge of the power of colour.

There are traditionally accepted seasonal colours and monthly weekly even daily colours.

Many New Age therapists are now using this knowledge in Colour therapy – this is not new!

Lets start with the seasonal colours.

Samhain (New Year)	Brown/Black
Yule	Red/Gold/Green/White/Evergreen
Imbolc	White/Green
Spring Equinox	Green/Pale blue/Pale yellow
Beltane	Green/White/Pink/Red
Midsummer	Red/Yellow/Orange/Blue
Lammas	Orange/Yellow
Autumn Equinox	Orange/Brown/Red/Yellow

Monthly

November	Brown/Black/Grey/Purple
December	Red/White/Green/Gold
January	White/Grey
February	White/Green
March	Green/Pale colours
April	Green/White/Pink/Yellow
May	Pink/Red/White
June	Green/Red/Pink/Blue

July	Yellow/Blue/Green
August	Red/Yellow/Orange
September	Brown/Gold/Orange
October	Brown/Black/Gold/Red

Daily

Saturday	Grey/Purple
Sunday	Yellow/Gold
Monday	White
Tuesday	Red
Wednesday	Orange/Yellow
Thursday	Blue/Silver
Friday	Green

Colours are used in many different ways. Here are some of them:

1. Altar dressing. ie. using a seasonally appropriate item of the relevant colour. E.g. Autumnal leaves at Samhain.
2. Power dressing, i.e., wearing something of the appropriate colour for that day/month/season etc.You'd be amazed to know who practises power dressing. Keep your eye out in the news!
3. Altar clothes/Tarot silks/Rune silks etc
4. Interior design. Dare I say it? Feng Shui.
5. Luck, e.g., if you were born in February for example you might find it lucky to wear a piece of Green jewellery.
6. Divination by simple coloured stones.
7 Magical purposes, i.e. candle magic.

Remember always: magic encourages us to use our imaginations. Thinking things through and making connections between the purely symbolic and what you feel it relates to is a key to greater understanding.

6

Simple Smudging

The purpose of smudging is to clear a building, room, or space that you wish to work in, of negative energy.

Step 1

Collect your goodies.

You will need:

A smudge stick and smudging feather or you can use charcoal & incense
Charcoal tablets (Available at most new age or occult suppliers)
A small heat proof bowl
Enough earth or sand to half fill the bowl
Frankincense resin (Or oil if you can't get resin)
A pair of tongs
A naked flame

Step 2

Holding the charcoal tablet with your tongs over the naked flame, wait until it spits and starts to go red, then place it in the pre-prepared bowl. Onto it, place a few grains of incense and take it to your first room to be smudged.

Step 3

Leave the bowl in the room making sure to shut all windows and doors.

Go away for 10 minutes and visualise yourself protected by a violet light all around you.

Step 4

Return to the room and remove the bowl to the next room. Keep repeating this ritual until all rooms independently are done. Through rooms count as one.

Step 5

Cover the bowl with earth to put it out. Starting with the first room go round the house opening all the windows and doors.

WARNING Clouds of billowing smoke will now emit from your house and some bright spark may ring the fire brigade. To avoid this, keep an eye outside in case anyone shows an interest. Whilst the smoke is going out visualise all your negativity going off with it and think *My house/room is now clear.*

Step 6

After about ten to fifteen minutes you should be able to close your windows and doors again. Then take a deep refreshing breath and feel the difference.

Smudging shouldn't be necessary too often but it has its uses, as I'm sure you will find.

7

Simple Candle Magic

This is really the easiest type of spell to cast.

You will need a candle of the appropriate colour. (To choose the colour either use one that matches the season or the theme of your spell e.g., for love use pink.)

If all you have is white that's fine. Some witches like to stick to beeswax candles, it's up to you and obviously you need a candle-holder. Some oil to anoint your candle is very pleasant, as with candle colour you need to choose a suitable oil for your spell.

Now all you require is a quite place where you know you won't be disturbed for about half an hour. If it is daytime then close the curtains. Find a comfortable position to sit in facing your candle and light it. Now whilst focusing on the candle take several long slow breaths and feel yourself relaxing. Try to empty your mind of distractions and just focus on the flame. Your breathing should be quite normal and relaxed.

Imagine yourself surrounded by a violet light that will protect you from harm.

Stay focused on your candle and start to imagine whatever it is you want from this spell coming true. Visualize your spell becoming reality. After a little while take one deep cleansing breathe and if you can safely do so leave your candle to burn right down. (Don't worry too much if you can't). The violet light will fade on it's own it is not necessary to get rid of it in your mind. Believe it or not you have just completed a simple spell.

As a rule, if the spell doesn't appear to have worked there may be a number of reasons.

1. You may need to do it for several days on the trot to get a result.
2. Impatience, sometimes it takes a little longer than we want for things to occur.
3. Have you chosen the correct moon phase? Remember, waxing draws to you, full ok for most things except banishing, waning gets rid of things.
4. Did you break the golden rule: *harm none*?

Practise this on simple things first.

8

Spells

Exams

Moon phase; Waxing & Full

Whilst studying try holding a piece of Amethyst in your hand. It will act as a memory cell, i.e., it may remember even if you don't think you will. Also try having a lighted candle anointed with lavender burning in the room. Avoid the candle catching your eye though or it will act as a distraction. The lavender will calm and centre you, which should help with concentration. If you find lavender soporific then try a nice zingy fruit oil of some sort. If you wish to you could concentrate on asking for an appropriate ethereal source to help you in your studies. Merlin is a good choice.

Affirming before you start: *I will understand, I will remember, I love (subject);* is very beneficial also.

Take your amethyst to the exam and hopefully it should help activate your subconscious memory.

Don't expect miracles. If you haven't studied there will be nothing for your higher self to remember in the first place.

Spots

Moon phase; waning

Firstly give up using soap on your spotty bits. Try adding a little sea salt to your bath water instead. If you shower just use shower gel or soap on the bits that matter and avoid getting soap on the spots. After washing light a white candle, imagine a protective violet light around you, and visualise yourself with perfect skin. Repeating a mantra whilst focusing on the candle will help.

e.g. *May I please be blemish free.*
These spots they are now history!

Making up your own mantra is better though.

The best cure is fresh air. Avoid over washing. Stop picking. Forget them and they will forget you.

Love

Moon phase; Waxing & Full

Using the simple candle magic technique, a pink candle, rose oil, flowers for your altar, begin by visualise the type of person you want to attract. Then either using a previously written verse or poem or whatever you feel like saying at the time focus on the candle and send as much love as you can muster into the universe.

Your mantra could be something like this: *Loving soul, hear my call, come to me.*

Another well-used method is to pick the first hawthorn blossom you see and put it on your altar. It must stay alive for three days and nights. If you are meant to have new love it can happen very quickly.

Money

Moon phase; Waxing & Full

Again use candle magic and dress your altar with either crystals (especially citrine) or a few coins. Visualise yourself finding a way you want to earn money. Yes, we are sorry, but you have got to be prepared to work for it. Wishing for the winning lottery numbers will not work, there would be a lot of pagan millionaires if it did.

If you are too young to work then asking for a pocket money increase is ok.

Guess what! Yes, there is a mantra to use again, e.g.; *A job I need to pay my way, May it bring happiness everyday.*

Crazy though it may seem burying some money in the garden also helps.

Weight

Moon phase; Waning

Eating healthily is **the** most important consideration. This spell **will** be rendered useless if you are not. You should also be taking regular exercise as any good witch does anyway. You can use the same technique as the spot spell but obviously change the mantra to maybe: *May I be the shape I want to be, a happy, fit and healthy body.*

Another way of approaching it can be to get a doll and dress it with as many layers as it takes to resemble the shape you are now. Put the doll in the kitchen to keep an eye on you and hold it during your ritual. Afterwards you can remove a layer. This spell is best repeated for at least a week. Before you decide you need to loose the weight ask your mother or doctor first.

Bullying

Moon phase; Waning

This is an all too common problem. Magic for this kind of problem should only be tried when all else has failed. Has it? This kind of spell comes under the heading of banishing. Again stick to your candle magic but remember you must not wish the bullies any harm. The best way of approaching it is to firstly get yourself some protection, symbolic of course. Various crystals are protective such as tiger's eye. Blackthorn is a traditional tree for this and a wand fashioned from this is a good idea. Try to obtain it before it starts to bud.

When you meditate imagine yourself surrounded with blackthorn and chant a mantra as usual. E.g.; *Bullies of bullies leave us be, from your torment set me free.*

It is interesting to note that most bullies are being bullied themselves. Think about it.

9

Incense, Herbs and Oils

Incense

Incense seems to be a vital part of ritual and certain smells can have a strong effect on our moods. It can be helpful to burn some incense when you are meditating as well, as long as you know what you are using and what its effects are likely to be. Remember that any sort of magic opens your psychic faculties and if you use inappropriate incense, you may well end up with a thumping headache.

You can easily make your own, this way you will know exactly what has gone into it and if you enjoy making things, you can use it as a way of making good presents for fellow pagans. Always keep notes of what you have put into incense and the quantities.

There are many ways of tackling incense. Some people collect lists of planetary or zodiacal herbs and spices and mix the incense up according to those. Others might take a theme, like the Greenwood for example, and work on that. Decide what you want the incense for and then gather your information.

To make any sort of scented substance, you will need three levels of smell. The low note, usually produced by resin or some woods, a middle note, which is produced by bark, leaves and some woods, and a high note which comes from flowers and leaves and such things as lemon oil from the skin of a lemon.

Here are a few simple ideas for you to work on. Read up the subject and experiment. You will find that frankincense will make an appropriate base for almost all mixtures:

The Sun – Ash leaves, lemon balm, bay leaves, cedar wood, cinnamon, marigold, orange blossom (philadelphus will do), sweet marjoram, gum benzoin and frankincense.

The Moon – Hyssop, jasmine, lilac, Madonna lily, night scented stock, rosemary, violet, myrtle and bay leaves.

Mercury – Cinnamon, hazel, lemon rind and leaves, lily of the valley, mace, marjoram, primrose, honeysuckle and sandalwood.

Mars – Cypress, carnation, garlic, Hawthorn blossom, musk and magnolia.

Venus – Apple blossom, clematis, coriander, roses, saffron, sandalwood, stephanotis and thyme.

Jupiter – Basil, beech, cloves, jasmine, lavender, nutmeg, oak and sage.

Saturn – Benzoin, cumin, cypress, frangipanni, pine, rue, blackcurrant and elder berry.

There are a whole host of other plants you can use, check them first in case they are poisonous or you could cut short a promising magical career! If you pick plants, only take what you actually need, ask the plant spirit first and thank them afterwards for their gift, which to them is a sacrifice.

Oils

Aromatic oils heated in a burner are a really good way to produce uplifting smells. You can mix up to 4 or 5 oils, more than that starts to get unpleasant. The easiest and most straight forward oil to use is frankincense which is very pleasant, quite strong and as you don't need more that about 4 drops in the oil burner it is a fairly economical way to achieve a good result. You won't produce clouds of smoke either.

Never leave an oil burner alight in a room unattended, the same goes for candles

Your family won't be pleased if, after invoking the Goddess or the fairies, you then burn the house down.

Aromatic oils are very powerful and can have a marked effect on our mood and feelings. If they are the wrong ones they can also make you feel very unwell, so get a good book on the subject and read it up first. Oils such as lavender, orange, lemon and lemon balm, geranium and rosewood are all good to use.

Herbs

This is a huge subject. All witches make the knowledge of herbs an integral part of their studies and use them for all manner of things. Herbs are used in medicines and cures, creams and lotions, incense and cooking and in an assortment of magical techniques. If you want to use them it is essential to study the subject properly. It is fine to have a more superficial knowledge for making charms and incenses or herbal items like lavender bags or lavender bottles. If you want to use them for healing then you must know what you are doing. There are very good courses that teach herbalism and if you want to prescribe for other people you will have to become a properly qualified herbalist.

Having said all that, there is a lot that you can do with herbs without having to study for several years and you can really get down to earth – literally – in growing different plants, making things and using them in magic.

10

Trees and their Significance

Trees are highly important to witches and pagans in many ways. For a start trees provide an oxygen cleaning service to the world, they also provide shelter, fuel, fruits and nuts, furniture, fencing – you name it and there is likely to be a tree involved somewhere.

A great many of the old magical religions have trees as a central symbol. The Shamans often use a tree as a symbol to help them in their trance work, the Norse religion sees the various levels of life as being on the great World Tree Yggdrasil, Qabalists use a diagram called the Tree of Life and it crops up all over the world in folk decorations and embroideries.

The ancient Celts took trees very seriously and used them as guides in a magical alphabet and a calendar. There were two major groups of Celts who migrated to the British Isles who brought their tree alphabet with them. As they were widely separated in time the alphabet changed and the one that is usually used nowadays is called the Beth, Luis, Nion, after the first three letters. The other version is called the Boibel, Loth. In both cases their names are exactly like ABC.

A simple form of the Celtic Tree Calendar and Alphabet is given below with the dates that are usually ascribed to them. If you want to study this further there are several books available, the most important being The White Goddess by Robert Graves.

Some people have developed extensions of this alphabet, putting in the vowels that we use with their own trees and special days. However, for most purposes it is enough to use the calendar as it stands.

Table 1

Letter	Name	Tree	Dates	Quality
B	Beth	Birch	Dec 24–Jan 20	Beginnings
L	Luis	Rowan	Jan 21–Feb 17	Sensing
N	Nion	Ash	Feb 18–Mar 17	Moving
F	Fearn	Alder	Mar 18–Apr 14	Choosing
S	Saile	Willow	Apr 15–May 12	Believing
H	Uath	Hawthorn	May 13–June 9	Cleansing
D	Duir	Oak	June 10–July 7	Strength
T	Tinne	Holly	July 8–Aug 4	Sacrifice
C	Coll	Hazel	Aug 5–Sept 1	Inspiration
M	Muin	Vine	Sept 2–Sept 19	Excitement
G	Gort	Ivy	Sept 30–Oct 27	Renewal
NG	Ngetal	Reed	Oct 28–Nov 24	Unexpected
R	Ruis	Elder	Nov 25–Dec 23	Continuation

One way of using trees is to consider which qualities each tree stands for and as you go through the year to try to express that quality throughout the relevant month. It is an exercise that will give you considerable new insights into yourself.

The Celts also had a form of divination called Ogham (pronounced OH AM) in which trees and letters were used as guides. This consisted of lines carved above, below or through a line or the edge of a stone or piece of wood.

In the Norse religion the runes are each assigned a tree; to a certain extent they are similar to the Celtic tree lists. Compare the tables and see what you can make of the similarities or differences between the Norse and Celtic ideas.

If you want to make something practical using a significant tree you could start of by making a magical wand. The best idea is to decide what qualities the wand will represent to you. You should also have a definite idea about the system you will be using, for instance, Norse or Celtic and the type of wood you want.

Table 2

Rune	Tree	Element	Deity	Colour
Feoh	Elder	Earth/Fire	Freya	Fiery red
Ur	Birch	Earth	Thor	Dark green
Thorn	Oak/Hawthorn	Fire	Thor	Bright red
Os	Ash	Air	Odin	Dark blue
Rad	Hazel/Oak	Air	Forsetti	Bright red
Ken	Pine	Fire	Freya	Light red
Gifu	Ash/Elm	Earth	Odin/Freya	Deep blue
Wyn	Hazel/Ash	Fire	Baldur/Freyr	Gold
Haegl	Yew	Water/Ice	Urd/Hel	Pale grey-blue
Nyd	Beech	Fire	Skuld	Red/Black
Is	Alder	Ice	Verdandi	White
Ger	Apple	Earth	Sif	Yellow-gold
Eoh	Yew	Earth	Hel	Dark blue
Peorth	Ash/Beech	Water	Norns	Black
Eolh	Ash/Yew	Air	Heimdal	Rainbow
Sigel	Juniper	Fire	Baldur	Gold
Tiw	Oak	Air	Tiw/Tyr	Bright red
Beorc	Birch	Earth/Water	Frigga	Dark green
Eh	Oak/Ash	Earth/Air	Freya/Freyr	Light blue
Mann	Holly	Air	Heimdal	Deep red
Lagu	Willow	Water	Njord	Deep green
Ing	Apple	Earth/Water	Freya/Freyr	Yellow-green
Odal	Hawthorn	Earth	Odin	Deep green
Daeg	Alder	Fire	Heimdal/Baldur	Red

Then go out into the countryside and look for your wand. Make sure that you know what trees you are looking at. You will probably find a suitable branch lying on the ground. Check to make sure it is not rotten, some types of wood, such as birch, rot very quickly once they have fallen. Don't go hacking at the trees. For a start they don't like it. How would you feel if someone came along and started hacking at your arms with a penknife? Added to which the tree will probably not belong to you. Also, leaving an open cut on the branch may well allow disease to get into the tree. So it is better to pick up a fallen branch. Very often you can look really hard, find nothing and then when you have given up in disgust and are just about to go home the perfect piece of wood suddenly appears in front of you. You will know when you find the right one.

Depending on how you want your wand to look, which will also depend on what sort of magic you intend to do, you can either leave it natural or you can strip the bark off, dry it, polish or wax it or even paint it with significant symbols. Some people add crystals to their wands, coloured ribbons, beads, shells or fir cones. All these will depend on how you think your wand should be. This should be entirely your own decision, ignore anyone who helpfully says, 'Oh, no, that's all wrong, it ought to be...' It is **your** wand and sums up **your** ideas.

11

Sacred Places

A sacred space is, in essence, anywhere that you feel is special and which helps you feel more connected to the spirit both within and without. You may already have a special place that you already visit. You may decide to use your bedroom as your sacred space or another room in the house. If you decide that home is best then it is very important to smudge the room you will be using to remove any lingering negativity. This can be done very simply but it is a bit smelly so check with your parents first. For instructions on how to do it see page 22.

If your garden lends itself to working undisturbed this can be a lovely place to use, or anywhere suitable outside is great!. You can have as many sacred places as you wish or you may want to stick to one its up to you.

When starting out it is a good idea to get back to nature. There are however very few truly natural places left to visit but if you root around you should be able to find something. If you can't find anywhere natural then a man made park or forest will do.

As long as the place draws you to it and makes you feel calm, peaceful and yet energised by being in it then that's fine. For circle or group work you definitely need to find somewhere that you won't be disturbed which is why most people these days prefer to work indoors, its warmer too.

Unlike other belief systems pagans these days don't go round erecting huge stone circles (more's the pity), or obviously marking places to worship. We go to where we feel we should and sometimes you will be put onto places by other pagans in your area. It is of course very important to avoid trespassing on other people's property and if you use a public place make sure you minimilize your environmental impact on the place, i.e. don't litter, that is very un-pagan. Although the lighting of fires is very tempting unless you really know what you are doing or have permission it is not generally advised to do so, accidents do happen, and also it makes you very obvious.

Once you start to explore your own doorstep from a pagan point of view you will be surprised by what you can find. Many Churches were originally built on pagan sites and some still have some evidence, i.e. circles, green men, runic markings etc.

Once you have discovered a special or sacred space it will draw you to it, so be prepared for regular visits. The more you get to know your sacred places the more invaluable they will prove to be to you as visual aids in meditation or path-working for example.

Remember if you need to take something from your sacred space etherically or otherwise always leave a small appropriate offering, biodegradable of course.

Most of all, use it well.

12

The Green Man

Many of us have heard of The Green Man but not everybody knows who or what he is. In simplistic terms he is thought to be the spirit of the woods. His origins are probably pagan. As to exactly when his images first appeared, who knows?

Green men faces appear mainly in churches and cathedrals all over Europe and the British Isles. One interesting observation made by Cannon Albert Radcliffe of Manchester cathedral is that on average, where they occur, Green Men faces outnumber images of Christ by a staggering 12-1. There are hundreds of them in Britain alone but no one seems to know why.

So, is he an early Christian attempt at denouncing the wild and primitive side that is in all of us? Or is he there to pacify and honour this ancient nature spirit?

No documentation remains, (if indeed there ever was any), to prove his origins.

He is a real mystery. Were early Pagan/Christian converts too frightened *not* to give him life? They may have appeared to have succumbed to the idea of Christ as a saviour but were they ready to sacrifice their intrinsic link with nature's spirit? I think not.

It would appear then, that the early blending of Christianity and Paganism met with some conciliatory gestures, such as, allowing the spirit of the trees into their sacred space. Considering early churches were, at least partly, constructed from trees this was probably a wise move.

Up until 1939, nobody had actually given a name to all the many and varied "tree faces" that adorn the churches. It was a Lady Raglan that first linked them all up under the banner of Green Men.

The common characteristics visually are a man's face (usually) emerging from a sea of leaves. Some have leaves "growing" out of the mouth, ears or nose. Some grin, some frown, some grimace and some look at peace. Many good examples can be found at Canterbury Cathedral, Kent; Fountains Abbey, North Yorkshire and the infamous Rosslyn Chapel, Edinburgh, which boasts 103 no less. There really are too many to mention but you are sure to find you have them locally if you live in Britain, or Europe. If not, you'll have to visit us.

The Green Man is also one of our most common public house names. Often found on pubs that are in or near to existing, old woodland.

What is he? He is Pan, Cernunnos, Puck, Robin Hood or Jack 'o' the Green amongst others. He is wild and free, an untamed spirit. He is nature and man blended in perfect harmony. He gives life to fertility and is pretty sexy too. He is the spring God calling the young maidens to the forest to dance. He is the thrust of new spring growth, the product of the previous season, fresh and green reaching for the light.

He is the spirit of potential new life. So, all in all, he is a pretty busy chap!

He is gaining in new-found popularity. People from all walks of life regardless of age or belief system are waking up to his and other nature spirits messages. People are losing faith in science and worried about the damage inflicted on nature. His message is again finally being listened to. Luckily there have always been some that have never lost the contact. They have helped to keep him alive. Pagans, obviously.

One lasting tradition that has connections with him is Beltane. This is the May Day festival held in towns and villages all over the British Isles. Men don antlers and leaves and lead the May Day pageant. Morris dancers dance for the general fertility of the season ahead.

Robin Hood and Maid Marion really are the archetypal young God and Goddess. Their story evokes all the images of a Beltane celebration. They live the high life in the woods protected by the nature spirits, and their own wits. They turn away from greed and suppression trying to free everyone from tyranny. They delight in simple pleasures and share everything equally. Dancing feasting, drinking and yes, probably sex too.

At the very least the Green Man is with us to keep Christians aware that nature is always watching them.

As for your journey with him . . .

That's for you to go out and discover for yourself.

13

Faerie Magic

"If you go down to the woods today you're sure
of a big surprise !" Quote Teddy Bear's Picnic.

Have you ever found yourself taken back to memories of your
childhood that seemed magical or special? Did these memories
sometimes include being alone even momentarily somewhere
very beautiful or natural? Did you ever feel as if eyes were
upon you? Did the air somehow seem clearer and yet for a
brief time feel as though you were separated from the rest
of the world? Were all your senses stimulated simultaneously?
It may have felt like you were intruding on someone's privacy.
Were you struck by extreme fear and you didn't understand
why?

If your answer to one or any of the above was yes, then chances
are you have had a close encounter of the faerie kind. Literature is
bestrune with them, Peter Pan & Tinkerbell, The Tales of
Narnia, Grimm's Fairy Tales, A Midsummer Night's Dream to
name but a very few. We frequently indulge children in their
world and yet as adults we forsake them.

Some of us, albeit discreetly, have kept the connection going.

I was extremely lucky as a child to have some wonderful
natural woodland on my doorstep.

It came complete with ponds, islands, a grotto, a building we
called the Temple, bluebell woods etc.This, despite being in
London, was and still is, a very magical place.

Perhaps you had somewhere special like this near you as a child. Maybe it was your own garden or someone else's. Most of us had somewhere.

You can of course encourage little folk into your own garden. By keeping a wide variety of trees, shrubs and flowers and a few little Faerie toys you can make a start. They do like toadstools, ponds, little dark corners or better still a cave. They will not appreciate pesticides, weedkillers, rubbish or vehicles.

A pretty organic garden with quiet spots that are left for the most part undisturbed will work well.

Like everything in magic they have their dark side.

One of the most common occurrences is to be out walking (usually a spot you know well) and you find yourself inexplicably lost. It may almost feel as though the landscape itself has changed. This is commonly known as being Pixie Led. Don't under-estimate them. They will keep you confused for hours if they fancy. The crosser you get, the more geographically challenged you are likely to become.

The best bet is to laugh out loud turn three times clockwise and hope for the best.

There is an old wives tale that advises the wearing of your outer garment inside out as protection against Pixie magic. Mmmm.

If you start to stray into an area little folk are protecting then watch out for the warning signs.

Expect many a lash of branches or bramble, the sting of the nettle, a swarm of bees.

No matter how careful you are, if they want to have you they will.

If your presence is strongly opposed to then Faerie terror can strike. Once experienced it is never forgotten, allegedly. Apparently it is a sudden overwhelming fear for no accountable reason whatsoever.

I advise you to always respect this and head back. There may, after all, be a good reason for them putting the fear into you. They are sometimes given credit for warning you of even worse ahead were you to proceed, ie. a raving mad psychopath on the loose, or a dangerous precipice.

They may simply want us to butt out.

Nursery Bogies were in part invented by parents to stop children getting lost but one wonders if they have subsequently manifest themselves to look out for little ones who stray? Maybe.

Every now and then we are allowed a glimpse of their world. The veil parts and we see them peeking from behind a tree or bush. We may even be privileged to witness a Faerie dance.

It is said if you sit under a crab apple tree on midsummer's night you will see the king of the Faeries go by. There are so many types of little folk to see. Faeries obviously, Goblins, Elves (black & white), Pixies, Sprites but not Gnomes. Gnome or *genomus*, means earth dweller or simply earth, i.e. an elemental force. Offering gifts especially stones, money, crystals to the gnomes will help with prosperity.

If you want to connect with this very special and powerful magic then it would be wise to take these points into consideration:

1. Think like a child.
2. Have love in your heart.
3. Make your intentions pure.
4. Take an offering.
5. Carry some protection. Roses or rose oil is good.
6. Minimilize your environmental impact.
7. Believe!
8. Don't stare if you see something. It offends them.
9. If you find a small black stone out of place pick it up. This is a faerie stone it will bring you luck.
10. Be very respectful or else.

So what is Faerie magic?

I believe it's about connecting with them on different levels and letting them decide the magic for you but, there are Faerie spells you can do if you want. However that is a book in itself and there are a good few already to choose from. Sorry.

At its best Faerie magic inspires us creatively and helps to keep the wonder of the inner child alive in all of us.

Best Faerie days are: Imbolc Beltane, Lammas, Samhain, May Eve, Midsummer's night.
Best Faerie hours are: Dawn, noon, twilight, and midnight.
Moon phase: Full.

A little child,
A limber elf,
Singing, dancing,
To itself.
A Fairy thing,
With red round cheeks,
That always finds,
And never seeks,

Samuel Taylor Coleridge 'Christobel'

"If you go down to the woods today,
You'll hardly believe your eyes!"

14

Ritual Feasting

Suitable things to eat for a festival or ritual can be a bit daunting. There are several cookery books about seasonal or ritual feasting but they often suggest rather more than you might want to prepare. I think it is usually enough to have a plate of small cakes or things to nibble which are appropriate for the time of year. Here are some ideas and a few recipes. Look for other recipes. Hot Cross Buns are, of course, readily available in the shops but you might like to find a suitable recipe and make your own.

Imbolc – Almond Cakes or Barley and Honey Cakes

Almond Cakes
8 oz self-raising flour, 1 egg, 4 oz caster sugar, a little milk, 8 oz ground almonds, 4 oz margarine, 1 teaspoon almond flavouring.

Rub the margarine into the flour to the very fine breadcrumb stage, stir in the sugar and ground almonds. Beat the egg lightly with the almond flavouring and 4 tablespoons of milk. Stir into the dry ingredients and mix to a light, creamy dough. Use a little more milk if necessary. Put small spoonfuls into paper cake cases and bake in a hot oven. Do not burn the tops. Sprinkle tops with finely chopped almonds if you wish or a mixture of almonds and sugar.

Beltane – Hot Cross Buns (sun wheels), Cheese Cake

Cheese Cake
This doesn't need cooking but you should make it, if possible, a day in advance as it needs time to set.

8 oz digestive biscuits, 3 oz butter (melted), ¼ pint milk, 8 oz cottage cheese, 2 oz sugar, thinly peeled rind of one lemon, 11 oz can mandarin oranges (drained and 3 tablespoons juice reserved), ½ pint double cream, ½ oz gelatine (this is 1 packet of ordinary gelatine or 2 packets of vegetarian gelatine), 2 egg whites.

Break up the biscuits, reduce to crumbs in the blender or put in a paper bag and bash with a rolling pin. Mix with the melted butter and press into an 8 inch loose-based cake tin. Put in the fridge to set.

Put milk, cottage cheese, sugar and lemon rind into the blender and blend for about a minute. Add the mandarin oranges (minus a few for decoration) and blend again for half a minute. Whip the cream until it is thick and quite firm, fold into the cheese mixture making sure that it is all nicely mixed (no lumps!). Meanwhile dissolve the gelatine in the leftover mandarin juice in a bowl over a saucepan of hot water. Make sure that the gelatine doesn't get too hot. Then stir into the cream cheese mixture.

Whisk the egg whites until they are very stiff and fold into the cream cheese mixture. Pour into the tin with the biscuit base and put in the fridge so that it sets.

When set, take it carefully out of the cake tin and put it on a plate, decorate with the remaining mandarin pieces if you wish.

You can use other sorts of tinned fruit, which will give a different colour to the cheesecake, for instance, loganberries will make it pink. This will make quite a large cheesecake and it is very rich.

Lammas – Apple Cakes, Saffron Buns

Apple Cakes
2 medium sized cooking apples, 8 oz wholemeal flour, 6 oz butter or margarine, 2 – 4 oz brown sugar, 1 beaten egg, a pinch of salt, 1 teaspoon ground cinnamon, 1 teaspoon baking powder.

Peel and dice the apples. Mix the flour, salt, cinnamon and baking powder in a bowl and rub in the butter or margarine until it looks like fine breadcrumbs. Add the other ingredients and mix together well. Put rounded spoonfuls into paper cake cases in a baking tray and bake in a moderately hot oven for 20–25 minutes. They should be a golden colour, cover during cooking if they start to get too brown. You can use up eating apples that have gone a bit soft for this but the buns may be a bit sweeter so you might need to use less sugar.

Samhain – Gingerbread Men, Shortbread

Shortbread
8 oz butter, 4 oz caster sugar, 4 oz cornflour, 8 oz plain flour, pinch of salt.

Cream the butter and sugar until white and fluffy. Sieve the dry ingredients together and gradually add to the creamed mixture. Knead until smooth. Press into a 12 × 8 tin (or a round sponge sandwich tin) and smooth the top with a knife or the back of a pudding spoon. Mark into fingers or petticoat tails and bake in a slow oven for 30–40 minutes. This is a very delicate mixture and will brown very easily so cover it during cooking if it starts to look golden. When cooked take out of the oven and re-cut the fingers or tails and dredge with sugar whilst still hot. Leave until cold and then remove from the tin.

Moons

For ordinary full moons and new moons you could make short-bread biscuits cut into crescents and full moons. There are a great many other appropriate food possibilities so try what you like from the suggestions I have made and then see what else fits in to the season you are celebrating. Fruits, nuts and salads are also very good as well as eggs in the spring. Crumpets are often eaten as full moon food – being round and white – there is really no limit to what you can try.

15

Ritual Drinking

When you are doing a ritual or celebrating one of the eight festivals you may feel the need for a suitable drink. In a lot of books on witchcraft you will find the mention of 'cakes and wine', 'cakes and ale' or 'mead and meat'. They all seem to be heavily alcoholic. If you don't need or want to drink alcohol but want something that is traditional or appropriate to the time of year here are some suggestions. Try them out and see if you like them or use them as a starting point from which you can think up other recipes. Feel free to alter them or use other mixtures if you like.

Imbolc

This is the time of year when lambs are being born and in ancient times, when people drank ewe's milk or goat's milk much more than cow's milk, it was the time of year when milk was again available. You could try sheep's milk although both it and goat's milk have quite a strong flavour if you are used to cow's milk. As the weather is still usually very cold one possibility is to have warmed milk with cinnamon and a little sugar mixed into it. You can experiment with the spices – cloves, mace, cinnamon and nutmeg might all be suitable. You could try using honey instead of the sugar and this would give a very comfortable taste to the milk.

An alternative if you don't like milk is to put a quarter of a block of softened creamed coconut into the liquidiser with two ripe bananas and a couple of tablespoons of hot water. Whizz this round in the liquidiser until it is completely smooth and a little bit frothy. It is rich, warming and delicious.

Beltane

This is the time of year when life is really energetic and fast moving. You need a light, energetic sparkling drink. Try mixing a cup of orange juice, a cup of grapefruit juice – or a couple of tablespoons of fresh lemon or lime juice – with a couple of cups of old fashioned lemonade or fizzy water. Put some early lemon balm leaves in the drink and leave them for 10 minutes to float around and infuse it with their scent.

Lammas

This time of year is when the plants have done most of their work and there is a feeling of relaxation in the earth. The fruits are ripening, there is plenty to eat and people are lazing around in the hot sunshine. For this time of year you need a drink that symbolises the richness of the season. Use mango juice mixed with pineapple juice or liquidise fresh strawberries with raspberries or another fruit you like, perhaps blackcurrants. If you are liquidising fresh fruit you may need to add some carbonated or still water. Add a spoonful of warmed honey and stir well if you like sweet things. Chill it for a while in the fridge and then drop in some borage flowers, thin slices of orange and possibly a cherry or two. This should be rich and full of summer sunshine.

Samhain

For this we suggest Hot Fruity Punch which is a great favourite with people in the cold winter months and has a definitely festive feeling to it. A great many people are convinced with this one that they are drinking something very alcoholic and it gives them a delightfully wicked feeling; give it to your elderly relations and see their eyes sparkle! You will have to adjust the quantities to suit your taste.

A box of red grape juice, about a teacupful of grapefruit juice, half a teaspoon of mixed spice or a mixture of cinnamon and clove. Put all the ingredients into an enamel or other non-metallic saucepan and warm it through until it is quite hot. Do not boil as this spoils the flavour and texture.

The drinks you have at your festivals and rituals should reflect the season and mood of the occasion. There is scope for lots of experimentation, enjoy trying new tastes and flavours.

16

Tarot

The wonderful world of Tarot is shrouded in mystery and super-stition.

There is no doubt at all to those who study and work with Tarot that it works.

It is wise to remember, however, that it is a powerful tool and can easily be misused.

Perhaps you are thinking of buying a set, or maybe you are just tempted to have a reading? Be warned. Tarot gets to the root of your personality and exposes your weaknesses as well as your strengths. It also explores your possible futures. I say "possible" as I believe we all have the will to change our own destiny on a conscious level and it is the things that happen outside this level of control that we have to deal with whether we like it or not.

To be successful at Tarot reading you really need to keep an open mind and most importantly be true to yourself. For example, if a picture suddenly pops into your head that seems to have come from nowhere, tell the questioner what you see. This nearly always has some significance.

A popular misconception concerning buying Tarot cards is that it is unlucky to buy your own. Rubbish. It helps if you choose them, you are more likely to get a set you can actually relate to.

There are 78 cards in a true Tarot set which are divided into 22 major arcana and 56 minor cards.

The only real differences between sets are the themes and the artwork.

All other types of cards are simply divination sets. Some people find Tarot is not for them and may well find that they will click better with one of these instead.

I'm not going to tell you how to read Tarot: there are plenty of good books that can do that. The best way to do it is simply to meditate on a card a day and write down everything the card seems to mean to you. You'll be surprised at the results.

TAROT

The Major Arcana

The major cards number 22 from 0 to 21 in totality.

The major cards represent life's journey. All of us will encounter each aspect of these experiences before we complete our incarnations.

They vary in interpretation depending on their position and the other cards surrounding them. Each of the major cards does however present itself as quite an important point in our lives where it is important to take stock and really investigate their meanings to us.

Let us start our journey with:

0 The Fool

A carefree young man looks about to start out on one of life's great adventures.

The journey starts with the need to explore our surroundings. This is the same as a baby exploring his world. It may mean that it is time to take a risk. It's time to shake off the old and start something new and exciting. It does however advise against naivety. Safety should be considered. He represents the child within all of us. Sometimes it is good to let that child out to play.

1 The Magician

A male figure pointing above and below forms the central theme of this card.

The four elements are surrounding him.

The potential inside the egg of the Fool has cracked and the potential for growth and revelation is exposed. The magician basically says anything is now possible. Just choose your goal and I will help you on your way. It indicates exciting times ahead when adventures will beckon. It will be a time when your sixth sense will be trying to work in your favour so any intuitive feelings should be listened to.

2 The Empress

A blossoming mother figure surrounded by nature's bounty.

She is a powerful symbol of fertility. She can of course also mean the reverse, infertility. Usually though she reveals a fertile and creative side to all of us and encourages us not to waste our creative juices so to speak. She represents pure female energy and can relate to hereditary matters i.e. family. Birth, marriage, abundance; all these things are the Empress.

3 The Emperor

An older male figure usually sat on a throne, holding a symbol of lightning in his right hand. The Emperor is wise and solid. He has recognised the need for firm structure to our lives. He encourages routine and hard work. He relates to long term security and common sense. He represents male energy and a father figure in our lives.

4 The High Priestess

A mystical woman usually dressed in white seems to be almost hovering.

This card relates to female intuition. She helps us when we need our sixth sense to be working well for us. She encourages us to trust our gut instincts. She can pop up to warn us that a secret is about to be revealed. She is a shadow though and although there is potential in her wisdom it is rarely used to its fullest. She also means an inner journey to maybe even the darkest corners of our souls.

5 The Hierophant

Priestly looking chap this one, usually holding a scroll.

He is what you expect him to be. He is encountered when we are spiritually in need of a boost. He wants us to journey with him if not in a spiritual sense then at least in a philosophical way. He tries to connect between worlds and reaches towards the gods. He is a builder of bridges and reconciliation, and warns that a valuable lesson is about to be learnt.

6 The Lovers

A young couple or a man having the choice of several lovers.

This card usually indicates a romantic possibility or maybe more than one. Whatever the choice it warns us to be careful in our decisions over love.

Although we may choose to trust our gut instincts sometimes they are not really listened to. Basically I like to think of this card simply as, that first infatuation or the tension building between the sexes and definitely "think before you leap".

It can also relate to infidelity.

7 The Chariot

Surprisingly this is usually a picture of a man riding a chariot. There is a black horse and a white but they a both pulling in opposite directions.

A time when you will feel torn in two and may well have literally a 50/50 decision to make. A struggle will soon commence and although it could get very tense you will pull things back on track and all will be well.

8 Justice

A woman usually dressed in white sits on a throne between two pillars.

She has a sword in her right hand and an owl sitting on her left shoulder.

She represents a clear and if necessary, detached personality. She employs logic and reason in making clever and strategic decisions. Fairness is important and a balanced mind. Justice can mean a number of things, legal implications, a battle where intellect will win the day, emotional detachment, objectivity, rationality, honesty.

9 Temperance

A young maiden with wings stands over water. She is pouring water from one jug to the other. She appears introspective and whimsical.

This card represents a time when it would be detrimental to keep still, whether physically or emotionally. It can also be a time when the veil between worlds will be thin and it is possible to find yourself spending too much time daydreaming. She invites us to explore our feelings and allow them to flow. She teaches us that as well as being able to balance our thoughts we can also do this with our emotions. This helps us to avoid over reacting to situations. It is the card of compromise.

10 Strength

A figure (usually male) wrestling with or appearing as a lion.

This indicates a time when courage and strength will be tested. As well as an outer struggle of some sort this can also mean an inner fight as well. Sometimes we need to re-connect to our beast within and be really brutal to win either a moral or ethical battle. It is the inner strength we all possess but rarely need to use. An exhausting period.

11 The Hermit

A dark figure hooded usually carrying a scythe in left hand and light in the right.

A time of solitude. Time to reflect and judge yourself in all honesty. A need to withdraw a little from people and concentrate on self-improvement. Time to meditate and enjoy getting to know yourself. For some it is an opportunity to rediscover your individuality and start to appreciate time spent alone instead of fearing it. It represents the light within the darkness.

12 The Wheel of Fortune

Usually a cartwheel being turned by a group of people. It indicates a complete change in ones fortune. This of course could be good or otherwise depending on your circumstances. It is also an opportunity to break a bad cycle and give up on bad habits. It will quite often feel as if a chapter of life is about to end. This card usually appears when a person has come to grips with how we influence our own lives with our every thought and action. Not always an easy one to accept. Traditionally a card of increased fortunes.

13 The Hanged Man

A man either hanging from a tree or tied upside down in some manner, but always from one leg. He rarely wears more than just a loincloth.

This card shows us that sometimes we have to make sacrifices in order for something better to happen. This can manifest itself in many ways such as martyrdom on a grander scale or simply giving up chocolate in order to lose weight. It also indicates time in suspension. Also it can mean that all we need to do is change our perspective over an issue to gain more insight into it. Time may stay in suspension for a while.

14 Death

You know this guy, he hangs out with war, pestilence and famine.

Although the imagery seems obvious most Tarot readers are reluctant to interpret this card in its literal form. It can of course mean simply, death. How it is relayed is the important thing. Most seem to opt for the end of an era scenario, i.e. something has come to an end in order for something else to be planted and grow. Acceptance of mortality.

15 The Devil

As with Death the imagery is obvious. Usually a Pan-like character with a male and female figure dancing at the end of strings he holds.

This card shows us our dark side. This is the side we would usually rather ignore or suppress. Frequently it means our dark side might be tempted out to play and we should be aware of the potential consequences. It can also mean that we have blocked our own path to success and have given in to self-sabotage. It also relates to sexual inhibitions and prejudices. Beware temptation may strike!

16 The Tower

This shows a tower or castle that although it appears to be under construction it is in fact hit by lightning. The tower forces us to realise that even things that are set in stone and impenetrable, are still at threat from the elemental forces. It means a time when all our preconceived ideas are about to be tested. Out with falseness and in with brutal truth. It can also be that a literal bolt from the blue is about to hit us. It insists on a complete change of course. At its worst it can mean total destruction.

17 The Star

This card varies considerably amongst packs but as a rule it always has a large almost biblical star in the sky as its focal point. It appears to tell us that all that is bad in a given situation has now passed and although the future may seem bleak it reminds us never to give up hope. It also tells us that if the universe does not recognise that you have a definite goal then how is it supposed to know what you want. We need our ambitions and goals and we need to keep our inner star burning brightly.

18 The Moon

Obviously the moon is the main theme of this picture and it is generally associated with the female. It quite often has Cancerian connotations and water.

This usually indicates a period of uncertainty and quite often, confusion. Difficulty in making decisions and a general feeling of moodiness. Sometimes it comes at a time when we need to realise the difference between what is real and what is illusion. Sometimes it tell us that we are self deluding. Luckily like the moon herself it is cyclical and we rarely get affected by this for too long. If this card comes up repeatedly for you as a result then you need *help*, possibly?

19 The Sun

Usually a young male figure glowing like the sun.

The sun represents the male energies at work in their purest form, i.e. to fertilise the mother, i.e. the earth. This therefore portends to a very fertile and successful enterprise. When relating to a struggle it means victory. If it concerns a romance it bodes very well indeed. As a result it can only ever be interpreted positively unless it is the only good egg in a sea of darkness. Then it can mean that it lessens the effect of the other cards.

20 Judgement

A stern male figure holding a twisted serpent around a wand looking down on tortured souls in judgement. This is the ultimate we reap what we sow card. It teaches us to take stock of our actions and draw honest conclusions. It can also mean that we are about to be rewarded for our actions. It helps us to reach the stage where we choose not to make any more mistakes and take more control of our own destiny. It can mean we judge ourselves and others too much.

21 The World

This card has a serpent circled round upon itself with either a figure inside or some sort of male and female images. The four elements are displayed also.

The world indicates that a cycle has been successfully completed. It may mean that it is maybe time to rest or start to plan your next move. On every level it is interpreted as completion. There is nothing more that can be done to change, improve, or remove what has been carried out. The "back where you started" card.

Tarot

Minor Arcana

These are divided into four suites as in playing cards. Many people use playing cards to this day.

Pentacles – Earth – Physical forms – Materialistic
Swords – Air – Inspiration – Thought
Wands – Fire – Passions – Energy
Cups – Water – Movement – Emotions

These go from Ace to Ten.

Court Cards

King, Queen, Knight, Page of each suite

I won't go into detail with the minor cards or it will have to be a book in itself!

What I will do is give you a brief run through the numerical significance of each card and leave you to study a pack and draw your own conclusions as to its specific interpretation based on what you already know and the other cards around it.

It is important to see if any one suite is dominant in a reading, i.e. mainly Cups would indicate an emotional period or relationships being prevalent etc...

Ace – Something sudden. e.g. Ace of Pentacles, sudden prosperity.
Two – Divisions or partnerships, e.g. Two of Cup, partnership/consolidating.
Three – Imbalance problems, e.g. Three of Swords, health problems, being picked on.
Four – Rest, balance, celebration, e.g. Four of Wands, party time!
Five – Loss, difficulties, hardship, e.g. Five of Pentacles, money loss, big bills etc.
Six – Achievements, balance, recognition, e.g. Six of Cups, rewards, romantic gifts.
Seven – Disruptions, obstacles, e.g. Seven of Pentacles, sacrifice of security to gain elsewhere.
Eight – Speed, moving forward, e.g., Eight of Wands, progress after delay, increases.
Nine – What will be will be, almost complete, e.g. Nine of Swords, pressure brought about subconsciously.
Ten – End completion, as good as it will get, e.g. Ten of Swords, end of pain and suffering.

There are slight variations between packs however so go by your guide book but most of all go by your gut reaction to each card.

The Court Cards

King of Pentacles – *Capricorn*, Solid, reliable, money minded, practical.
King of Swords – *Aquarius,* Intelligent, knowledgeable, teacher.
King of Wands – *Aries*, Enthusiastic, optimist, creative, impatient.
King of Cups – *Cancer*, Caring, nurturing, medical.
Queen of Pentacles – *Virgo*, Industrious, managerial, stubborn.
Queen of Swords – *Libra,* Cold, calculating, thoughtful, perfectionist.
Queen of Wands – *Leo*, Energy, intuition, attention seeking.
Queen of Cups – *Scorpio*, Proud, passionate, deep.
Knight of Pentacles – *Taurus,* Possessive, sensual, adaptable.
Knight of Swords – *Gemini,* Quick thinking, adaptable, communication.

Knight of Wands – *Sagittarius,* Adventurous, daring, trouble maker, accidents.

Knight of Cups – *Pisces,* New romantic involvement, seduction.

Page of Pentacles – News relating to money or property.

Page of Swords – Rows, upset, gossip, bad news.

Page of Wands – Good news, creative period.

Page of Cups – News of a birth, new feelings.

Tarot Spreads

1 card

(major arcana)

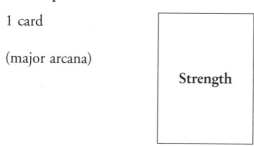

This is useful if you want a quick answer to a pressing problem, e.g.: Strength – a positive outcome is possible but not without a struggle.

3 cards

(all pack)

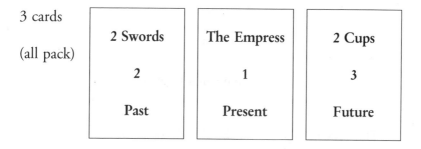

The three card spread gives you the past, present and most likely future of the situation, e.g.: the 2 of swords means that you are getting too involved in other peoples problems if you are not careful they could become your own. This is followed by the Empress, who urges you to be positive and creative in your response, keeping a feminine perspective. The future is the 2 of cups signifying that emotional harmony will follow and you will be getting on better with someone who affects you on an emotional level. The outlook in general is good.

5 cards

(all or just the majors)

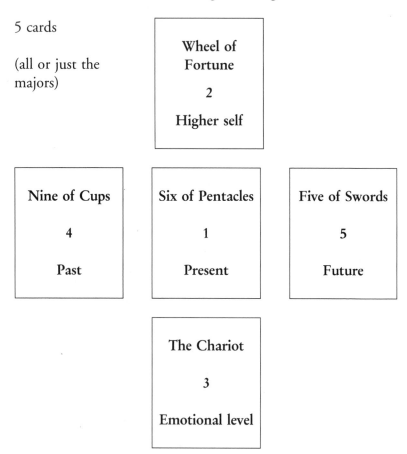

Wheel of
Fortune

2

Higher self

Nine of Cups

4

Past

Six of Pentacles

1

Present

Five of Swords

5

Future

The Chariot

3

Emotional level

The present represented by the six of pentacles is a financial problem that will be helped by someone you know. On a higher level the Wheel of fortune urges you to be more aware that you need to do more to help yourself and make the most of this improved situation. The chariot on the emotional level shows that despite feeling conflicts within, you should be able to pull things back on track and keep moving forward if you see challenges as progress towards greater understanding. The nine of cups in the past means that a wish came true because it was from the heart. The future as shown by the five of swords warns that you must live up to your responsibilities and you may need to swallow your pride to enable your wish to really come to fruition.

These easy spreads should get you started. Try not to refer to the cards for every tiny thing. That is not really what they are for. Stick to fairly major questions and you should be fine.

17

Other Forms of Divination

Divination, or Fortune Telling, doesn't only consist of Tarot cards and Crystal balls. Some people really can't get on with them but there are lots of other ways to look ahead, see what the possibilities are and make decisions about your life.

Dowsing

One method is to use a Pendulum. This is simple, direct and doesn't need expensive equipment but it does mean that you have to think about your problem and put it into a clear, unambiguous question.

The actual pendulum can be as simple as a ring tied to a piece of thread. There are a great many on the market, some cost a lot, some are quite cheap. Get one you really like. Many people have a crystal pendulum and they find that the combination of crystal power and their own mind power work well. Practice on simple things first, ask questions that you will find the answers to very soon – and write down the question, answers and the date and then check up to see how accurate you are getting.

Before you start you have to decide which way the pendulum will swing for YES and NO. Usually it swings in a clockwise direction (deosil) for Yes and in an anti-clockwise (widdershins) direction for No. However, some people find it works the other way round and sometimes you may find that it will change, this can be very confusing, so before a session of dowsing, check to see what the pendulum is up to. This is useful as it gets you into gear for the actual work you want to do.

It is very important to phrase your question very clearly and very positively. What you are really doing when you are dowsing is asking your subconscious a question. The subconscious is a very old and very primitive part of our mental equipment and it doesn't understand the word No or anything put in a negative way. So make sure you put your question in a positive way. "Is it going to rain tomorrow?" will get a sensible straightforward answer, however, if you ask, "It isn't going to rain tomorrow, is it?" what your subconscious will understand is, "It **is** going to rain tomorrow." and will answer accordingly. Always avoid the word IF in a question when you are dowsing, as it almost always suggests that you are in fact asking two questions at the same time. Take your time, divide it up and ask both the questions separately. That way you will get a much clearer answer.

It is a good idea to have a clear picture in your mind of what you are asking but be careful to avoid asking questions that you especially want answered one way. To get reliable results you need to be involved but detached from the outcome. It is a knack and comes with practice but it isn't always easy.

Dowsing can be used for all manner of different things – finding water, people, things that are lost, answering questions and medical diagnosis. If you enjoy using this method, there are many specialist books around and an organisation called the Society of Dowsers who could provide more information if you want to develop this skill. The great thing about it is that it is so simple. You can put your pendulum in your pocket and take it with you everywhere you go.

Runes

Runes are another form of divination. The runes are simple letter shapes that were devised by the Scandinavian people about 1,500 years ago. The simplest form of this system contains 24 letters, each has a meaning and it seems a fairly limited system at first sight. However, if you work with the runes you will find that each letter contains a wealth of meaning behind the obvious one and, of course, as with any divination system, they call different interpretations out of you according to the reading you are doing and the circumstances.

You can buy ready-made sets of runes or you can make your own. If you decide to take up the runes you might want to make a set in wood, for which you will have to see the article on trees in this book, or else collect small stones and paint the letters on them. However, a good way to start is to get a sheet of thick card from a shop that sells artists' materials. Cut it into 24 squares about $1\frac{1}{4}'' \times 1''$ square and carefully draw one rune on each square. Some people paint them in different colours and there are various opinions about what colour to use. To begin with I think a black felt tip pen on white card is good. You can always get into the colour complications later. The main thing is to get on with the method and see if you like the runes. You can consecrate your runes if you feel this will help.

The runes and their meanings are as follows:

(I have used the Anglo-Saxon names for the runes, other books may use slightly different ones.)

Rune	Name	Key word	Meaning
ᚠ	Feoh	Cattle	Wealth, success, fire, money, fulfilment
ᚢ	Ur	Wild Aurochs	Strength, luck, health, persistence
ᚦ	Thorn	Giant/Thorn	Sudden awakening, a thorn, destructive changes, fertility, protection
ᚩ	Os	God	Communication, the mind, learning
ᚱ	Rad	Wagon/cart	Journey, physical or spiritual
ᚲ	Ken	Torch	Creative fire, destruction leading to new growth, attraction

Rune	Name	Key word	Meaning
X	Gifu	Gift	Gift, union, sacrifice, a kiss, trust
Þ	Wyn	Joy	Joy of life and harmony, true will
Η	Haegl	Hail	Wild power, rapid or destructive change that is outside your control, past events
✝	Nyd	Need	Conflict, confusion, delay, the needs that drive you forwards, future events
I	Is	Ice	Time of waiting, stillness, stasis, winter, events now
♦	Ger	Harvest	The turning of the year, harvest, birth and rebirth, peace, reaping rewards
Ι	Eoh	Yew tree	Letting go or ending of events – as after the harvest, also protection and immutability of fate
Κ	Peorth	Dice box	Roll the dice, womb, matters that are still hidden, Wyrd, finding your path
Y	Eolh	Elk	Protection, continuance through the group, spiritual awakening, learning, the crow's foot
Σ	Sigel	The Sun	Success, protection, warmth and growth, energy
↑	Tiw	Victory	Trust, justice, courage, fighting for a just cause, masculine energy
Β	Beorc	Birch tree	Birth, renewal, new growth, promise of new beginnings
Μ	Eh	Horse	Union, relationships, change, fertility – physical and ideal, movement and change on inner levels, hidden knowledge
Μ	Mann	People	Social structure, groups, deep wisdom within the group/family/clan
Γ	Lagu	Water	Emotions, go with the flow, female intuition, vitalising energy of water

Rune	Name	Key word	Meaning
◇	Ing	Fertility	A doorway, the seed of something, pregnancy, vulva, sacred power of female sexuality
◊	Odal	Home	Ancestral land, inheritance, enclosure, homeland, family, inherited wealth
Ⴇ	Daeg	Day	New dawn, transformation, new beginnings, the place where opposites meet.

Keep your runes in a cloth bag.

A simple but very effective method of getting an answer to a question is to mix up the runes in the bag and draw out three without looking to see what they are. Lay them out in front of you, side by side. You can use this method to give you the Past, Present and the Future, or the Situation, the Action Needed and the Outcome. There are any number of possible combinations and ways of approaching problems. Try these out and see what else you can think of.

The Yes/No method is useful for a quick answer. Draw three runes as before and lay them out, side by side. If they are all upright the answer is Yes, if they are all upside down the answer is No but if some are reversed and some are not then you must read the meanings of the three runes and work it out.

You can also try casting the runes on to a cloth. Lay out a clean white cloth on the table and take all the runes in your cupped hands whilst you concentrate on your question. Cast them onto the cloth so that if possible they fall in a line away from you. Those closest to you are the past/present and as they move away from you they are steadily moving into the future. Only read the runes that are face up. Special attention should be given to runes that lie on top of other runes. This is a method that is worth working on as you can get an accurate measure of time as well as a sequence of events. As with any system, this one needs practice. You must become familiar with the runes and their relationships to each other.

Three Stone Divination

This is one of the very oldest and simplest methods, used by our ancestors thousands of years ago. With practice it can tell you a surprising amount.

First go out and find, or buy, three stones: a white one, a red one and a black one. They should all be about the same size, about the size of a large marble. Ideally you should find them yourself but you can also buy tumble polished stones that will work well too and will be attractive and smooth to handle. Make a small cloth bag to keep them in and when you have a query, make sure the answer will be of the Yes/No/Don't Know variety. Put the stones in the bag and mix them up whilst concentrating on the question. Pull out one stone. If it is white the answer is Yes. Black says No and Red says Maybe, Possibly or Don't know. With practice you can get more information out of this. If you cast the stones onto a table or the ground you can see which lands closest to you – that being the strongest influence, modified by the others. They might all fall close together, they might fall wide apart, one might be close to another – all these will modify the meaning. The method will also help to develop your intuition so that you will be able to use this simple system but get a lot of information through it.

Any system of divination is simply a way of gaining access to your own inner knowledge.

If you approach it sensibly and don't get stuck in superstition you will find divination a great help in assessing situations and people and suggesting courses of action. However, the final decision is yours. Nothing is ever absolutely definite in divination. The method you use will show you the options and it is up to you to make it happen if you wish to, but you have to decide. It is never the pendulum, runes or stones' *fault*. All they can do is show you how things look at the moment when you ask your question. The rest is up to you.

18

Romantic Sun Signs

You probably already know what star sign you were born under. This is known as your sun sign. There are twelve signs of the zodiac and each one gives you a generalised view of your most obvious personality traits. Just in case you are not too sure which one you are, here they are.

Aries 21st March–April 20th
Taurus April 21st–May 21st
Gemini May 22nd–June 21st
Cancer June 22nd–July 23rd
Leo July 24th–August 23rd
Virgo August 24th–September 23rd
Libra September 24th–October 23rd
Scorpio October 24th–November 22nd
Sagittarius November 23rd–December 21st
Capricorn December 22nd–January 23rd
Aquarius January 24th–February 22nd
Pisces February 23rd–March 20th

The twelve signs are also divided into three groups of four. These represent the four elements of earth, air, fire, and water.

Earth people are sensualists. They react mainly to their five physical senses. They are realists and normally very grounded.
Air people are of the mind. Thoughts, ideas, inspirations and communication are what motivate them on the whole.

Fire signs are divine sparks. Energy is their bag. They are passionate creatures and their passions keep them driven. A fire sign lacking a passion is simply a pilot light on hold.

Water signs are controlled by their emotions. Feelings, theirs and others, are what make them tick. They react strongly to the moon's influence and are often described as moody.

Most astrologers have a pretty good idea as to which sun sign combinations work best both as friends and as romantic partners. As a rule you are most likely to get on with one of your own elemental group i.e. water/water. I think that air and water also mix well. As do fire and earth. Armed with this information you can now go ahead and see what the potential love of your life is like and how to go about catching them.

ROMANTIC SUN SIGNS

Aries

March 21–April 20
Symbol – Ram
Fire – Cardinal
Tarot – King of Wands

What Are They Like?

People born under Aries are full of enthusiasm. They are impulsive and passionate.

Although they have a reputation for being warlike, this usually only amounts to an occasional flare up. They have endless energy and make good leaders. They are very ambitious and can be very much all or nothing people.

Boredom affects Aries very negatively. They can be impatient and easily irritated.

There is a tendency towards selfishness.

In short they are very creative, active people who are intense about everything they do!

To Catch Aries

Pamper that ego. Centre the conversation around them and their achievements. Compliments work wonders with Aries. Make them feel important. They are very much the children of the zodiac so be a little bit obvious. Dress seductively, smile, and listen. A love of the great outdoors is an advantage.

To Keep Aries Interested

To keep up with Aries you must have stamina and a desire for a deep and intense relationship. Give them room to breathe but when you do appear have a smile on your face. Laziness and depression are a huge turn off for Aries. Be affectionate, supporting and chilled. Aries are terrible flirts and not past the odd diversion, so keep that fire burning and develop a thick skin. Appeal to their sense of equality rather than trying to compete.

Taurus

April 21–May 21
Symbol – Bull
Earth – Fixed
Tarot – Queen of Pentacles

What Are They Like?

People born under the sign of Taurus are sensuous and down to earth. They are practical and dependable. They have a methodical approach to work. They are usually patient and dislike being rushed. Stability appeals to Taurus. They can suffer from jealousy and have a tendency to treat everything, including relationships, as a possession. They want lots of security and often get it. Stubbornness is a problem.

To Catch Taurus

This beast responds best to touch and smell. Scents will help and being tactile even in a simple innocent way will stimulate the bull.

If that approach doesn't appeal then seducing their stomachs often will. Treating them to a delicious meal is a real sensual treat to Taurus, backed up with a subtle aroma and the odd inadvertent touch will drive them crazy.

To Keep Taurus Interested

They are very sexually driven so be prepared for hours of canoodling. Offering to give them a massage is an alternative. They are pretty easy to keep really unless you go frigid on them. Watch out for the jealous streak though. Flirting with others will not be appreciated. They really are very simply pleased and in return offer stability and security so if you want to feel safe stick with Taurus.

Gemini

May 22–June 21
Symbol – Twins
Air – Mutable
Tarot – Knight of Swords

What Are They Like?

Gemini is a restless soul. They flit about never feeling settled. Being sociable and on the move appeals. They are usually a bit eccentric and this frequently expresses itself in their appearance. They love light-hearted flirtations but rarely mean anything by it. They know a little about a lot but don't often settle at anything long enough to be real experts at anything. They often spread themselves thinly and if anyone is likely to double book themselves it's a Gemini. Mental stimulation and intrigue is their bag so constant challenges and changes suit these characters.

To Catch Gemini

You will need an awfully big net. They really are the hardest sign to pin down. Sometimes their fear of being trapped will lead them into all sorts of deceptions and trouble. Be cool, really cool. Tease them. Reel in, then let go. Again, again they will cry. Keep changing. They need constant varied stimulation. Sometimes the speed of their reactions is awesome. Capture their minds first and the rest will follow.

To Keep Gemini Interested.

Security is a turn off for this sign. A life of travel and variety will suit. Show them you are stimulated by change. Suggest impulsive days out. Stand them up occasionally. They love being kept on their toes. Change your style and mood frequently. Possessiveness and jealousy have no room in this relationship.

Cancer

June 22–July 23
Symbol – Crab
Water – Cardinal
Tarot – King of Cups

What Are They Like?

Up and down mood wise. They are emotionally driven but rarely cope well with other people's emotions. They hate to appear vulnerable and have a tough exterior but a really soft centre. They love the whole idea of a secure family life but will only consider entering into it when they have the finances available to support it. They often hide their true feelings and create diversions to distract you from knowing what they really feel. They have a great quirky sense of humour and love to make you laugh. Laughter is their medicine in life. They love to nurture and often play both mother and father very well.

To Catch a Cancer

Distract Cancer from their worries and keep the laughter going. Be witty charming and attentive. Be consistent and strong. Appeal to the sensitive side on a non-personal level.

Show concern for others, adopt a whale, bring home an injured animal. All these qualities appeal to Cancer. Be assertive and honest. Overpower their senses, all of them.

To Keep Cancer Interested

Be tenacious. Be very, very honest but in a sensitive way. Show them you're taking them seriously and looking to the long term. The past affects Cancer deeply so be prepared to deal with someone with a long memory. Trust is a keyword with them so give it and be it. Be supportive, emotionally strong and sensual. Never ever try to make them jealous; they will snap viciously, run sideways and may never trust again.

Leo

July 24–August 23
Symbol – Lion
Fire – Fixed
Tarot – Queen of Wands

What Are They Like?

Big personalities, charming and romantic, that's Leo. They seem to be blessed with plenty of sex appeal so you could have competition. Whoever gives them the most attention will win. They can be easily seduced by expensive gifts and prefer a luxurious life style. Like Aries they have rather large egos so flattery will get you everywhere. They are a little superficial. Don't make the mistake of thinking this is a deep sign they are too tough for all that emotional stuff. If they are happy they will purr, if angry they roar and cuff. Life is for living and loving and they do it very well.

To Catch A Leo

They really can be terrible snobs so any hint at being important or famous or successful will appeal to them. Failing that be a bit flashy. They are suckers for a fast car or just an expensive look.

Be fashionable. Dazzle them with style. Add a bit of glitter and sparkle to your outfit. Talk about their favourite subject: them. Be seen in all the right and trendy places. They are usually real conformists. Even if you find an unconventional cat they will still want somewhere cosy and warm for all those *cat-naps*.

To Keep A Leo

Attention, attention, attention. That's all they really need. Loads of love and affection. Be prepared to run around after regal Leo. They don't expect to do much for themselves. They can be drama queens and are attracted to dramatic situations. Nagging will get you nowhere. Be bold and to the point. Avoid name calling and if you do win the argument don't push it any further. Just adore them and you'll do fine.

Be warned though, looking sloppy or generally letting yourself go is a particular turn off for Leos. Despite the fact their grooming is sometimes a bit hit and miss.

Virgo

August 24–September 23
Symbol – Lovers
Earth – Mutable
Tarot – Knight of Pentacles

What Are They Like?

Attention to detail is important to Virgo. They are generally tidy and organised people. They can be quite shy and unassuming. They have an intellectual mind and are very analytical. They can be a little puritanical. They don't usually care to be the centre of attention unless it's something they have really perfected. They are very easily embarrassed. They have the ability to switch off their feelings and get totally absorbed in their thoughts. They often set high standards for themselves and will frequently stay up all night if necessary to get the job done.

They have a habit of controlling the relationship without their partner even realising it's happening.

To Catch A Virgo

Approach them first as a serious friend then let things develop. Never trivialise a Virgo. They have rather conservative tastes so being flash is not a good idea.

Dress smartly and look interesting rather than loud. They appreciate subtlety and hate public displays both romantically and emotionally. They love being taken very seriously. They are very health conscious so being up on the latest nutritional information will interest them. They need lots of gentle appreciation.

To Keep A Virgo

Be prepared for a simple but easy life. Keep yourself fit and healthy. Joining a health club together will appeal. Keeping informed of current affairs and showing an interest in politics is useful. Weekend walks in the country helps them to get away from their serious side and helps them to relax. Approach them gently and cautiously but with a seriously romantic look in your eye whilst exposing your sexuality in a subtle way is a sure winner. Romance has to be private and intimate and in clean and fresh surroundings to get them going.

Libra

September 24–October 23
Symbol – Scales
Air – Cardinal
Tarot – King of Swords

What Are They Like?

On the surface they appear calm cool and collected but just like a duck appears on the water underneath they can be paddling like crazy. They are a pretty balanced blend of intellect and emotion. They are prone to confusion and inner conflicts in their attempt to keep their lives balanced. They can sometimes suffer from being in love with love. Looks can impress them but it must be balanced with a mature personality or intellect. Older Librans are dependable and secure. They can be infuriatingly indecisive. They mature well but can be fickle when young.

To Catch A Libra

Looks do impress at first so make your best effort. They like a well-groomed look. Scruffy unkempt looks are a turn off usually. They take time to grow up and will be prepared to play the field for quite a while. It's unlikely you will have a long lasting relationship with a Libran if they are young. Letting them think they have competition can help but could also upset their balance so tread carefully. They love obvious romantic gestures and gifts. They are easy to talk to and quick to understand.

To Keep Libra Interested

Look after yourself. Hair is a big turn on to Librans so regular visits to the hairdressers is essential. Try to avoid highs and lows. Balance really is their keyword. Always listen to their needs first and then get your own across. Share your time equally. If you want a night out with your friends Libra will expect the same in return. If you cook dinner Libra will often wash up without being asked. If a relationship based on equality is important to you, then Libra will try to provide it.

Scorpio

October 24–November 22
Symbol – Scorpion
Water – Fixed
Tarot – Queen of Cups

What Are They Like?

A deep and complex character. They come over as mysterious and have great insight. Their conversation is rarely light and you will find their eyes penetrating you for the hidden feelings within. They are cool on the outside but deep and passionate inside. They rarely expose their feelings until they feel completely under control of the situation. They are masters of deception. They are highly sexual but can be prone to excesses. They can suffer from moodiness only when they have worn themselves out trying to gain the upper hand in a situation.

To Catch Scorpio

Give an impression of danger and elusiveness. Be obviously sexy. Be very intense. Use your eyes: they have a magnetic appeal to Scorpios. Keep them guessing.

They love a mystery. Talk about deep philosophical issues. They are drawn to the forbidden so watch out!

To Keep A Scorpio

Be mysterious and elusive. Always let them think there are hidden depths of your personality they haven't discovered yet. Try suggesting a date with an adventure and hint of danger attached. They are very sexually driven and really feel their passions so be prepared to feel deeply in return. They have a reputation for revenge so tread carefully.

Sagittarius

November 23–December 21
Symbol – Archer
Fire – Mutable
Tarot – Knight of Wands

What are they like?

Optimists and extroverts. Travelling is their favourite pastime and freedom their key word. They are blessed with higher wisdom but don't always listen to themselves.

The expansive mind, they always see the bigger picture. They are cheeky and youthful and incredibly lucky on the whole. They have a tendency to try to be constantly on the move. They are terrible fidgets. They are outrageously generous and can be superficial. They do however suffer from foot in mouth disease which often stops them getting off first base in a relationship. Like Libra they get better as they get older.

To Catch Sagittarius

Don't bother just try and keep up instead. Be prepared to be on the move literally.

They are the gypsies of the zodiac. Responsibility with people is not their strongest point so if you want to pin one down try buying a puppy or any pet for that matter.

They love animals and have a real affinity with them. They tend to be a bit scruffy and disorganised so don't worry too much about dressing up for them. Be witty and intelligent. Sagittarius does not suffer fools.

To Keep a Sagittarian

Freedom is their key word. Allow them total freedom to explore any path they want and be prepared for the path to change at a moment's notice. Trust them and they will respect and trust you in return. Natural looks appeal so don't overdo the make up or dress. Be very open-minded and respect nature, this will earn their respect. Keep a first aid kit handy. All these adventures come with their fair share of minor accidents.

Capricorn

December 22–January 20
Symbol – Goat
Earth – Cardinal
Tarot – King of Pentacles

What Are They Like?

Romantically they can be shy and unsure of themselves. The business world is really their forte. If you have fallen for one of these it's likely to have happened at work or through work. They are so ambitious it drives them mad at times. They are the original workaholics. They are very money minded and great savers. On a personal level to hide their weaknesses they often hide behind a mask. This could take the form of a uniform or power dressing or make up. They are highly responsible and take life very seriously. They like dependable solid people.

To Catch A Capricorn

Be a bit showy with a hint of something sexy underneath. Clothes that look expensive but didn't cost a packet will impress. Offer security and fidelity. Constant admiration and lots of "Wows" go down well. They quite like being mothered so encourage them as you would a child. Being prepared to be their Rock of Gibraltar behind the scenes is bound to get their attention. Take the lead – sexually they can be a bit dense about who likes them at times. But give them space.

To Keep A Capricorn Interested

Respect admiration, love and appreciation are keywords to remember. Let them make all the major decisions. Nurture them but gently remind them now and then of your individual needs too. Let them know how much you enjoy their company regularly.

They can be exhausting so take time out to do your own thing while they are busy, busy, busy. Breaks away from work are essential but keep them short or Capricorn will drag work into every holiday.

Aquarius

January 21–February 19
Symbol – Water Bearer

Air – Fixed
Tarot – Queen of Swords

What Are They Like?

They have infinite curiosity and are generally very friendly. They love to try and get into your head and see what you are thinking. They are attracted to the unconventional and new experiences. They can be mentally exhausting. They have a tendency to treat all new relationships as some sort of psychological analysis. They frequently like to have fingers in lots of pies especially work wise. They are very honest and forthright. They flit between being very sociable but they do have quiet moments too.

How To Catch Aquarius

Be prepared to talk, talk and talk some more. Don't expect nights of wild passion although they can be very good lovers. Be prepared to experiment. Catch their eyes by being different. Crazy clothes and a rebellious streak all appeals to them. Have lots of progressive ideas and radical conversation up your sleeve. Brilliance impresses them the most.

How To Keep Aquarius

Be independent and definitely not clingy. Be well versed in at least a few subjects that they are not. Join a debating group or any group activity that involves heavy discussion. Let them be free to constantly explore new interests. Don't restrict them.

Deep meaningful passion is a huge turn off for Aquarius. Vary your dates and when the time is right for romance be interested in trying everything because they will.

Pisces

February 20–March 20
Symbol – Fish
Water – mutable

Tarot – Knight of Cups

What Are They Like?

Dreamers and ultimate romantics. Always looking for that perfect soul mate. They tend to view the world not as it is but how they would like it to be. They can be frequently disappointed in people and the world as a whole. They set high romantic standards and expect total loyalty in return. They are sensitive and tend to absorb other people's emotions like a sponge. Sometimes it feels as though the river of life is just a little too unpredictable for Pisces.

How To Catch Pisces

They tend towards infatuation quite easily so just hang around them long enough and they will be hooked or totally turned off. If they are not interested they are not afraid to speak their minds. Appeal to the child within. Pisces loves to play. They are real sensation addicts and can have addiction problems including getting addicted to people. The more disinterested you appear the more this fish will swim towards you.

How To Keep Pisces

Keep life romantic. They love that early relationship feeling. Lots of romantic meals, holidays, letters and attention should do the trick. They love to feel useful, it gives them great pleasure to give of their time for you on some errand or chore.

Pisces are often great DIY'ers. Vary every day in some way, and treat night times as a great romantic adventure, but watch out for their feelings.

19

Crystals

Crystals have become very popular and you can buy them in a great many shops. If you want to get the most out of them it helps to know which ones to buy and what to do with them.

Crystals have all sorts of uses. They can be used for healing, in which case you need to have some idea about the energy centres of the body – Chakras. You can use crystals as amplifiers of your own energy, some people use them in meditation, they can be used in shamanic drumming, and they can be used in witchcraft to contact the earth elementals and to focus the energy you are working with.

Here I had better explain that chakras – much talked about amongst the New Age fraternity – are centres of energy in the body. The Name "chakra" is Indian and in India the knowledge and use of the chakras goes back for thousands of years. If you want to study this bit of occult science in greater depth there are a great many books on the subject.

There are energy centres, or chakras, all over the body, in the palms of the hands and soles of the feet for example, but the seven major ones are situated in a line down the middle of the body and link up more-or-less with the endocrine glands. You will find them at:- the Crown of the Head, the Third Eye (between the eyebrows), the throat, the Heart, the Solar Plexus (midriff), the Belly (just below the navel) and the base of the spine.

They can be visualised as spinning balls of coloured light which are the "socket points" in the body where energy can be amplified or used for a particular purpose. Sometimes the body's energy becomes blocked or the flow can be sent off in the wrong direction by a shock, illness or some other event that can cause a malfunction (you can picture this as the electrical wiring of the body). When this happens, using crystals of the right colour and vibration can help to get the chakra functioning properly. As quartz crystals carry a tiny electrical charge and are live they are very appropriate for this sort of work.

Most people use Rock Crystal, which is also called Clear Quartz Crystal, for most things as it is an energetic stone that is open to almost all kinds of uses. The coloured stones tend to be more in tune with one or two particular energies and so have specific uses. You can use a coloured stone, Lapis lazuli for example, and enhance its effects by putting a rock crystal with it, boosting its energy level.

If you are using crystals in magic a simple and effective way is to go by the element you are working with. So if you are doing an earth based working you should use crystals and stones that are the greens and browns of the earth. A moon working would obviously benefit from Moonstone or Labradorite and a fire working would benefit from fire opal, if you can find some, or a fiery coloured stone, a very red Carnelian or an orangey Garnet would work well.

There are no hard and fast rules in working with crystals and often what works wonderfully for one person may not work at all for another. A lot of it depends on how you relate to the stones yourself.

Wearing stones to enhance the qualities of a particular Chakra is a popular way of using crystals. You can use the chart below to see which will suit you best. If you feel that two or three of your Chakras are out of balance you could string several appropriate stones on a chain or cord and wear them around your neck or wrist until you feel that the energies are back to normal.

Before you use a crystal you should cleanse and programme it. This is quite simple and the safest way is to use breath and light. Some books suggest soaking crystals in salt water but this can cause discolouration and damage to some very soft stones so start by trying this method.

Sit on a chair that is comfortable but doesn't allow you to slouch. You need to keep your back straight. Hold the stone you want to cleanse in your hands and visualise a huge globe of white light just above your head. Feel it pulsating above you and then let a beam of light come down, straight through your head, down your spine and down through your legs to the ground. As it goes feel it lighting up the whole of your body so that you are full of shining white light and energy. Then feel the energy, strengthened and enhanced by the power of the earth, come back up through you to join up with the globe of light above your head. See this loop of energy beginning to spin and feel it really getting your whole being full of life and energy. When you feel comfortable with this, and it does take a little practice, breathe a long breath on the stone. As you do so see the white light and energy being projected into the stone. The stone is being cleansed and revitalised with light, energy and breath. Three or four breaths should be enough if you do it with intention. Gently slow the spinning energy in your aura until it comes to a stop. Then feel it gradually returning down to the earth and up to the globe of light above you. When all is still again let the globe of light fade out and after a moment start to move about, stamp your feet a couple of times to get yourself back into the here and now. Your stone is now cleansed and ready for action. You should be feeling nicely energised as well.

You might want to programme your stone, once it is cleansed, and this can be done immediately after you cleanse it. Once the cleansing light has done its work, project into the stone the image of what you want it to do. It might be a healing stone, it might be a communication stone – what ever it is, project the image into the stone and then keep the stone for that use only.

These are just some of the most commonly used stones for the Chakras. There are plenty of alternatives and if you suddenly feel that a particular stone is right for a particular Chakra and no one agrees with you, follow your instinct, it is a more reliable guide than other people's ideas where it concerns you.

Chakras	Colour	Stones
Crown, top of head	White	Clear Quartz or Rutilated Quartz
Third eye, between eyebrows	Violet	Amethyst or Fluorite
Throat	Blue	Lapis Lazuli or Turquoise
Heart, centre of chest	Green	Rose Quartz or Green Jade
Solar Plexus, below breastbone	Yellow	Citrine, Aventurine, Tourmaline
Sacral, just below navel	Orange	Carnelian, Tiger's eye
Root or base	Dark red	Agate, Bloodstone, Haematite

20

Ancient British Festivals

We have already written about Quarter and Cross-Quarter Festivals from a magical point of view but a great many ancient festivals are still celebrated by ordinary people who have no real idea about the origins of the "bit of fun" they are taking part in. Some of the old festivals are almost the same all over the country – cheese rolling and hobby horse processions for example – and there are some that are unique to each town or village.

Most festivals are associated with the fertility of the land, the animals and the people, but some are specific. Such as fire festivals, and some later ones have developed as a celebration of the saint of a particular craft or skill – for example: St. Catherine's day in November, which is celebrated by lace makers. There are also very local celebrations where something such as Beating the Bounds was a traditional way of establishing the boundary of the common-land belonging to a village. This prevented arguments developing between communities.

When Christianity was trying to establish itself as the only religion at first the church tried to stop the people from celebrating their ancient festivals but after a while it was obvious that it would make life simpler and easier if the old festivals were incorporated into Christianity. Very often the old fertility celebrations were renamed and then carried on just as before.

A very popular festival which is nowadays the cause of huge amounts of enjoyment is Hallowe'en which was, of course, the start of the Celtic New Year and a time when the veil between this world and the others is thinned.

The stories of witches flying on broomsticks most likely comes from the practice of witches and shamans. They anciently used various herbal potions and salves in order to free their souls for a short while so that they could travel into the spirit world. Here they could find out the future for their community or get help for people who might be ill. They very often had the sensation of flying. Nowadays people have learnt techniques for travelling in the spirit world without needing to use any stimulants, as such practices can loosen the doors between this world and the spirit world leaving the witch in a very vulnerable situation.

The ugly masks that people buy for Hallowe'en are modern but the idea of being masked in a magical ritual is very old indeed; some of the reasons for wearing masks were to hide from unfriendly spirits or to lose one's own identity and take on another – which could also be that of an animal – or to identify with a particular God or Goddess.

The pumpkins that are so popular nowadays are a modern American invention but the symbolism is good. The round, orange coloured pumpkin is a very good sun symbol, hollowing it out and putting a candle inside reinforces the sun image and the scary face that is often cut into the side of the pumpkin can be seen to scare away evil in the face of the re-awakened light. Hallowe'en can be celebrated by Christians as well because it was turned into the Feast of All Hallows – or All Saints. Hallowe'en means the evening of All Hallows (Hallow meaning holy).

Another major festival that is still celebrated now, although in a rather scattered form, is Beltane. This is the great spring festival that balances Hallowe'en across the year. Beltane is the time of surging energy, creativity, physical desire and nature bursting out all over the place. The commonest festival associated with it is Easter but there are spring festivals of many sorts, all over the place, where fertility and new life is acted out and celebrated.

There is another fire festival and an old custom used to be to light two bonfires side by side and walk the cattle and sheep between them. The idea was that the fires would cleanse and invigorate them after the winter and they would become strong and fertile. Men and women would also leap over bonfires in an effort to encourage fertility. Beltane was also the time when young people would go a-Maying and often spent the night out in the woods. Babies born as a result of this celebration were not considered illegitimate. This was the one time in the year when May blossom from Hawthorn trees was allowed to be brought into the house. At all other times it was considered unlucky. All the traditional Easter foods were eaten at the Beltane festivities long before Christianity and the custom of decorating eggs to give to loved ones as presents goes back to the Stone Age.

Over time a great many of the old festivals disappeared but in the Victorian period some were revived by people who were interested in keeping their heritage. They saw it all being swept away by the development of industrialisation and modern ways of living. As people have become increasingly separated from the rhythms of life and the production of the most basic necessities – food and clothing – the meaning of the old festivals has become to a great extent irrelevant. However, those of us who are interested in remaining in touch with the rhythm of the natural world look at them in a different light.

Wherever you live there will be some traditional festivals and it is worth doing a bit of investigating. You can find out some surprising things about your local area in the process and almost everywhere in the British Isles has some secret history as well as a tradition of local ancient gods and annual festivals.

All over northern Europe there are similar festivals which stem from the same basic need that people felt to align themselves with the creative forces of the universe. If you travel around you may find that there are some differences of culture or climate but they are really quite small. The underlying message is always about the same needs and aspirations that our ancestors had and that they share with us nowadays.

21

Pagan Links and Websites

UK Pagan Links – **www.ukpaganlinks.co.uk**
Has contacts page, moots info and music, poetry, humour, clipart etc., info on magazines, info for young pagans, what's on etc.

Various useful links – **www.gmpsychics.co.uk**
very varied links – wide variety of subjects (a bit random though).

Pagan and Occult sites – **www.antipope.org/paganlink**
good place to start for pagan sites in UK & Ireland.

Inkubus Sukkubus – pagan rock group
Inky's official website –
wkweb5.cableinet.co.uk/sukkubus/inkubus.htm
photos, gigs, shopping etc.

Twisted Tree – **ourworld.compuserve.com/homepages/twisted_tree**
Info and links to other useful sites. Covers area (mainly) Glos, Wilts, Dorset, Somerset, Devon, Cornwall but links to other UK sites as well.

Pagan Federation – **www.paganfed.demon.co.uk**
International and regional UK links (the organisation has not been popular with younger pagans due to an apparently condescending attitude by older people. They are trying to put this right). Membership of PF only open to people over 18. The website does have good, and many, links though.

SpiritLinks – **www.spiritonline.com/links**
A massive number of mostly American sites aimed at teenagers who are beginning to get into wicca.

Teenage Pagan Sites Index –
www.witchvox.net/links
www.witchvox.net
Lots of sites, lots of info, worth a look, mostly American.

Irish Paganism – **www.paganireland.com**

Green Circle – **www.greencircle.org.uk**
Contacts group and a forum for esoteric discussion and the sharing of information.

Witches Tree – **www.witches.org.uk**
Female paganism, free Tarot and Rune divination, info on witchcraft, links etc.

Norse and Associated sites – **todd.reimer.com/norse.html**
Info on Norse mythology, gods etc. and some links.

Asatru (Norse paganism) –
www.religioustolerance.org/asatru.htm
Lots of info on Asatru and links

The Celtic Connection – **www.wicca.com**
Info, links, shopping etc.

Celtic Links –
geocities.com/Athens/Parthenon/3162links_pagan.html

Slavic Paganism and Witchcraft –
hometown.aol.com/hpsofsnert/index.html
Lots of info on all aspects, also Russian Pagan Tea Room Message Board, links to other sites such as Okana's Web.

Slavic paganism –
www.geocities.com/Athens/Atlantis/7308/slavic.html
Info, links etc.

Okana's Web – www.okana.net/page.html
Polish pagan site but has info on other Slavic and Baltic paganism, links etc.

The Solitary Practitioner's basic Guide to the Druids and Celtic Mysticism – www.uoguelph.ca/~bmyers/druid.html
LOADS AND LOADS of info.

The Druids – www.geocities.com/Athens/2519/druids.html
Lots of info, bibliography and druid-specific search engine and links to the rest of Lady Jen's website.

Greek Paganism –
www.geocities.com/Athens/Delphi/7969/greek_pagan.html
Info and links.

Mithraism – the legacy of the Roman Empire's final pagan state religion – x/europe/ancient_rome/E/Gazeteer/Periods/Roman/Topics/Religion/Mithraism/David_Fingrut**.html
A lot of info on Mithraism

Pawprints & Purrs – www.sniksnak.com/lore2.html
Lore of the cat – a lot of info about Egyptian cat worship.

Fellowship of Isis – www.fellowshipofisis.com
International org. dedicated to honouring the religion of the Goddess in Her many forms. Info, events etc.

Midgard's Web – www.astradyne.co.uk/midgard
Contact group, newsletter etc of the Norse religion.

SUGGESTED FURTHER READING

The Green Man by Mike Harding, Aurum Press Ltd, 1998

The Magic of Herbs by David Conway, Jonathan Cape, 1973

The Tarot Revealed by Eden Gray, Signet Books, 1969

The Complete Book of Tarot by Juliet Sharman-Burke, Pan Books 1985

A Practical Guide to the Runes by Lisa Peschel, published by Llewellyn Publications, 1999

Beyond the Yew Dale by Paul Sykes, The Little Black Dog Computer Company, 1994

Creative Visualisation by Melita Denning and Osborne Philips, Llewellyn publications, 1980

Tree Wisdom by Jacqueline Memory Paterson, published originally by Harper Collins, now Thorsons 1996

The Crystal and Mineral Guide by John Lee, Aeon Press, 1998

Celtic Magic by D.J. Conway, Llewellyn Publications, 1990

Norse Magic by D.J. Conway, Llewellyn Publications, 1990

The Ancient British Goddess by Kathy Jones, Ariadne Publications, 1991

The Norse Goddess by Monica Sjoo, Dor Dama Press/Meyn Mamvro Publications, 2000

The Witches' Goddess by Janet and Stewart Farrar, Phoenix Publishing, Inc/Robert Hale Ltd., 1987

Hedgewitch by Rae Beth, Robert Hale Ltd., 1990